the complete book of Soft furnishings

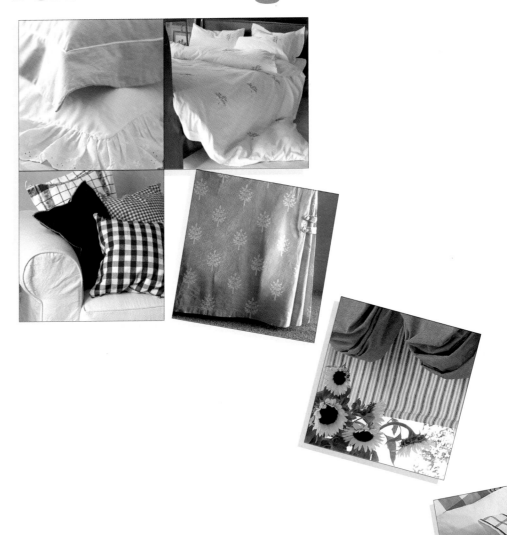

the complete book of
soft
furnishings

karen coetzee • rené bergh

photography by craig fraser

contents

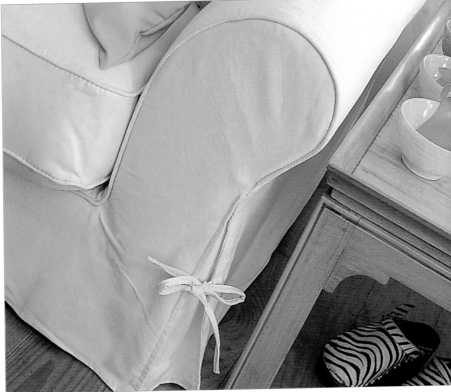

SEWING TECHNIQUES

TACKING (BASTING)

Tacking is used to temporarily hold together two pieces of fabric. Knot the end of the thread and then make long stitches just inside the stitchline, or set your machine to a long stitch and sew just inside the stitchline. Tacking stitches are removed once the seams are properly stitched.

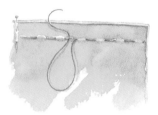

BLANKET STITCH

The easiest way to sew this stitch is to have the raw edges of the fabric facing your body. Work from left to right. Double-stitch at the left edge of the fabric to secure the thread. At the required depth and length of the stitch, push the needle through the fabric from the front to the back. Point the needle towards your body. Place the thread from the previous stitch under the needle. Continuing to work towards your body, pull the needle through the fabric, securing the thread under the needle to form a loop along the edge of the fabric. Repeat.

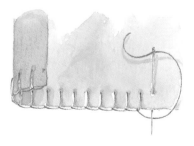

GATHERING STITCH

Gathering stitch consists of two parallel rows of long, evenly spaced stitches. If sewing by hand, make a knot or backstitch at the beginning of the first row to secure the thread, and then make generous, evenly spaced stitches. Leave a long piece of thread unsecured at the end. Do a second, parallel row of stitching in exactly the same way, making sure that the stitches and spaces in both rows line up. Gently pull the threads up to gather the fabric evenly, and then knot them together securely. If sewing by machine, set your machine to a long stitch, backstitch once to secure the thread and then proceed as described above.

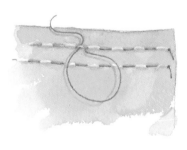

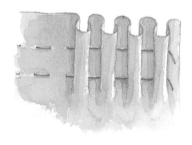

SLIPSTITCH

This stitch is used on hems and to sew linings to curtains. The secret to the success of slipstitch is to make it as invisible as possible, and to match the thread to the main fabric. Working from right to left with a fine needle, pick up a few threads of the fabric (A). At an angle, slide the needle about 1–1.5 cm (⅜–⅝ in) under the fold of the hem, and then bring it out to form a small stitch. Repeat.

SATIN STITCH

Satin stitch is a smooth, closely worked decorative stitch which produces a solid line or shape. To stitch it by hand, use embroidery thread and an embroidery needle. Mark the required pattern on the fabric. Secure the thread at the beginning of the marked line or shape. Sew each stitch very close to the next so that a solid pattern is formed, and stitch as illustrated.

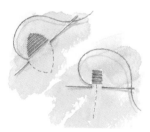

To stitch by machine, adjust your machine to the satin stitch setting, select the required stitch width and stitch carefully along the marked line.

OPEN (OR FLAT) SEAM

1
With right sides of the fabric together and raw edges aligned, pin and stitch 1.5 cm (⅝ in) from the edge (this is a standard seam allowance). Press the seam open and flat.

2
The raw edges may be finished off in any of the following ways:

a
Cut the raw edges with pinking shears to prevent fraying.

b
Turn under a small hem and stitch with either straight or zigzag stitching.

c
Overlock the raw edges together, or trim them to 1 cm (⅜ in) and zigzag them together. Press to one side.

FLAT-FELLED (OR DOUBLE-STITCHED) SEAM

1
With wrong sides of the fabric together and raw edges aligned, stitch 1.5 cm (⅝ in) from the edge. Press the seam open and trim one side only to 3 mm (⅛ in).

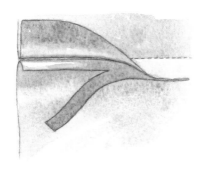

2
Fold the wider, untrimmed seam edge under the trimmed edge, enclosing all raw edges. Press carefully and then stitch close to the folded edge to finish off the seam.

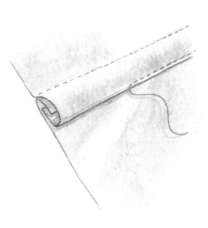

FRENCH SEAM

1
With wrong sides of the fabric together and raw edges aligned, stitch 5 mm (³⁄₁₆ in) from the edge. Trim the raw edges to 3 mm (⅛ in).

2
Turn the fabric so that the right sides are together. Press a neat edge along the seam line. Stitch 1 cm (⅜ in) from the pressed seam line, enclosing the raw edges. Press to one side so that the seam lies flat.

SNIPPING SEAMS

Snip the selvedges of a flat seam to prevent puckering.

Snip across the corners close to the stitch line to reduce bulk. Be careful not to cut too close to the stitch line, however, or the corner may be weakened.

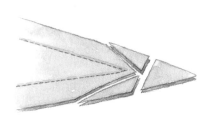

Snip notches into the seams next to the curves to ease tension. If the curve is very tight, snip the notches closer together.

FLAT BORDER

1

Cut border strips double the required width. Fold the edges to meet at the back of the border. Press carefully.

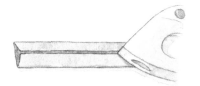

2

Attach the border by pinning, tacking and then stitching carefully along both outer edges. Stitch both sides in the same direction to prevent puckering.

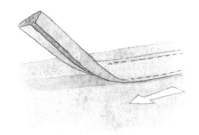

INSERTING A ZIP

1

Tack the seam closed. Establish the required location of the zip and mark the top and bottom points. Machine stitch the seam securely on each side of these marked points. Press the seam allowance open and flat. Position the zip centrally over the tacked seam in the marked location. Tack all around the edges of the zip to hold it in position.

2

Using the zipper foot of your sewing machine, stitch close to the zip all the way around. Remove all the tacking stitches.

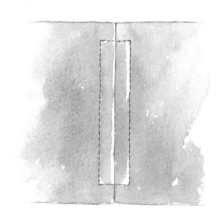

MAKING UP BIAS BINDING

1a
To mark the bias of the fabric, fold the fabric diagonally with the selvedge parallel to the top edge of the fabric. Mark the fold line.

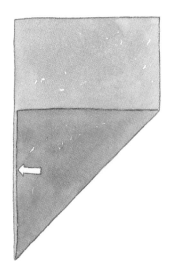

1b
Working parallel to this fold line, mark diagonal lines to form 4 cm (1⅝ in) wide strips. Cut out the strips.

2a
To join the strips, place the short edges right sides together at right angles with the raw edges aligned. Stitch.

2b
Press the seam flat and trim the overlapping edges.

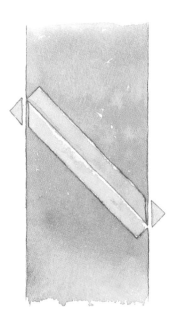

ATTACHING BIAS BINDING

1
Working along the top and the bottom edges of the strip of bias binding, press 1 cm (⅜ in) to the wrong side.

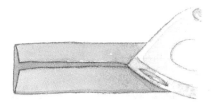

2
Open up the binding and position the right side of the binding on the right side of the fabric, raw edges aligned. Stitch along the pressed foldline.

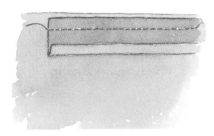

3
Fold the binding over the raw edges to the wrong side of the fabric. Pin and slip-stitch or machine stitch closed.

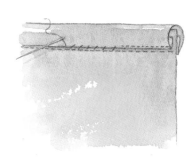

MAKING UP PIPING

Piping cord may vary in thickness depending on its intended use. Strips of fabric for the binding, wide enough to cover the cord and still allow a 1 cm (⅜ in) seam allowance on either side, must be cut on the bias.

1
Enclose the piping cord in the binding. Stitch closed, sewing close to the cord and using a sewing machine with a zipper or piping foot, or sew by hand.

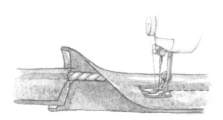

2
Where strips of binding covering the piping cord must be joined, fold under a small hem in the first piece and then overlap the second piece of binding with this folded hem. Stitch closed.

3
To join lengths of piping cord, when necessary, first fray a short length of each end piece, and then intertwine these loose threads, making sure that the join is the same thickness as the rest of the cord.

ATTACHING PIPING

1
With raw edges aligned and right sides together, position the piping on the fabric.

2
Pin and stitch close to the cord, using a zipper or piping foot.

3
When attaching piping to a curve or corner, snip the edges to ease the cord into position.

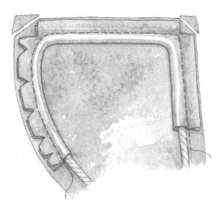

MITRING A CORNER

Mitring is a very neat way to finish a corner. This method of mitring is suitable for a corner that has even-sized hems on each side.

1
Press a double-turned 3 cm (1¼ in) hem on both sides of the corner. Fold open.

2
At point A, fold the corner diagonally and press. Trim the excess fabric.

3

Fold the side hems double so that the corner seams meet neatly.

4

Stitch the hems along the edges. Slipstitch the mitred corner closed.

MITRING A BORDER

1

Press 1.5 cm (⅝ in) to the wrong side along each edge of the border strip.

2

With the right side of the fabric facing up, the right side of the border facing down, raw edges aligned and allowing an overlap at the corner, position the border on the fabric. Stitch along the bottom pressed foldline, stopping about 5 cm (2 in) from the corner.

3

Attach the second side of the border as instructed in step 2.

4

Overlap the borders and mark the diagonal across the corner.

5

With right sides together, lift the two border strips and pin along the marked diagonal line. Stitch and trim excess fabric.

6

Turn the border to the right side of the fabric, and press the edges carefully.

7

Pin and stitch the border along the inside edges. Slipstitch the join closed.

FRILLS: CALCULATING FULLNESS AND FABRIC

Measure the required length of the frill. Multiply this measurement by two to two and a half (depending on the fullness required). Divide this total by the width of the fabric to determine the number of drops you will need. Multiply the number of drops by the width of the frill (including standard hem and seam allowances of 1.5 cm [⅝ in] each) to determine the amount of fabric required.

EXAMPLE

1 To make a 6 cm (2¼ in) wide frill for a cushion measuring 40 cm x 40 cm (16 in x 16 in), the required length of the frill is 160 cm (63 in)
2 160 cm (63 in) x 2.5 (required fullness) = 400 cm (157 in)
3 400 cm (157 in) ÷ 140 cm (55 in) = 2.86 rounded up = 3 drops
4 3 drops x 9 cm (3½ in) (width of frill + hem and seam allowance) = 27 cm (10¾ in) fabric required.

Note that if the frill has to be pattern-matched, refer to page 31.

MAKING UP A FRILL

1
Join the drops using open, overlocked or French seams, and pattern-matching if necessary.

2
Turn over a double 1 cm (⅜ in) hem, press and stitch.

3
Sew two rows of gathering stitches 1 cm (⅜ in) from the top edge of the frill.

4
Carefully pull up the gathers, spreading them evenly along the length of the frill.

5
With right sides together and raw edges aligned, place the frill and the fabric together.

6
Pin, tack and stitch between the two rows of gathering stitches.

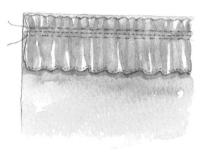

7
Once stitched in place, remove the gathering stitches.

8
Trim the raw edges and overlock, zigzag, blanket stitch or bind the edges together.

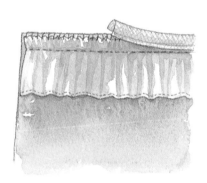

BOWS

1

Cut a strip of fabric to the required length and twice the required width of the bow plus a 3 cm (1¼ in) seam allowance. If required, shape the ends. With right sides together and raw edges aligned, stitch 1.5 cm (⅝ in) in from all the raw edges, leaving a 10 cm (4 in) gap unstitched through which to turn the sash right side out. Press the sash well and slipstitch the gap closed.

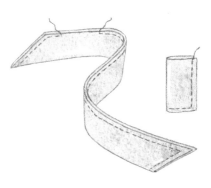

2

Using the same method, make a smaller strip. Its length should be double the finished width of the bow strip (the edges, however, will not be shaped).

3

Fold the sash to form a bow.

4

Use the smaller strip to secure the centre of the bow. Stitch closed at the back.

ROSETTE BOW

1

Stitch two identical strips of fabric as instructed for the bow on the left, but do not shape the ends. Turn right side out, centre the seams, and press.

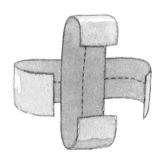

2

Place one strip over the other to form a cross, as illustrated. Fold all four end pieces to meet at the centre back, and stitch in place. Turn the rosette over and attach a button to the centre front.

COVERED BUTTONS

Buy the base of the covered button from any haberdashery or needlework store. These bases are available in different sizes. Some are made of plastic, others of metal: it does not matter which you buy as the method of covering the button remains the same. Use offcuts of the required fabric and, if necessary, make sure that any motifs will fall in the centre of the button. Or use contrasting fabric for a special effect.

1

Cut a circular piece of fabric with a diameter 1.5 cm (⅝ in) wider than that of the button. Tack all around the outer edge, leaving long threads unsecured at the beginning and end of your stitching.

2

Draw the fabric over the button top, pulling the loose threads to gather the fabric tightly. Knot the threads securely. Press the button back over the raw edges and clip closed.

APPLIQUÉ

Appliqué is the technique of sewing or attaching one piece of material to another to form a decorative pattern. Use a variety of colours, textures and patterns for a fun and exciting effect, or attach fabric shapes of the same colour but using contrasting thread for a cool, modern look. Make sure that all the fabrics used for appliqué are pre-shrunk, colourfast and fully washable.

1

Choose your motif. Cut out the required shapes, allowing an extra 1 cm (⅜ in) all round. Tack 1 cm (⅜ in) in from the edge around each shaped piece. Pin and then tack the shapes in place on the main fabric piece.

2

Enclosing the raw edges, satin stitch all round the edges to secure the motif to the fabric.

CHOUX ROSETTES

Choux rosettes are very easy to make. Use them to provide a finishing touch to grand window dressings, or stitch a rosette over the join of permanently fixed curtains, or at the top corners of an elaborate pelmet or swag and tails.

1

Cut a circle of fabric with a diameter two and a half to three times the required finished diameter of the rosette. Sew two rows of gathering stitches around the edge of the circle.

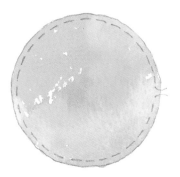

2

Gently pull up the threads to gather the circle, and then secure the threads.

3

Working on the wrong side of the puffy, balloon-like rosette, 'scrunch up' the fabric and make very small, random stitches to secure a fold here and there.

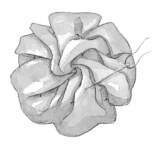

CALCULATING FRENCH PLEATS

When calculating and marking up pleats, work on one curtain at a time. Each curtain is pleated identically. Allow a 5 cm (2 in) overlap on each side of the curtain. Each pleat uses about 20 cm (8 in) and, as a guide, allow about 4 pleats in every 120 cm (47 in) width of fabric (if the fabric is wider increase the number of pleats). Pleats are usually spaced about 10–12 cm (4–4¾ in) apart with a pleat falling within the overlap at each side of the curtain. The rest of the pleats are evenly distributed between these outside pleats. This means that there is always one more pleat than there are spaces between pleats (for example, if the curtain has five pleats, it will have four spaces between the pleats). However, this is just a rough guide and the measurements must be adapted to suit your own needs. Remember that the total of the unpleated fabric (the overlaps and spaces) must equal the required finished width of the curtain.

1
Establish the required finished width of the curtain.

2
Multiply by two and a half to allow for sufficient fullness. This is the width of the flat curtain before it is pleated.

3
Subtract the finished width from the unpleated width to calculate the extra fabric that can be 'used up' by the pleats.

4
Divide the figure obtained by the proposed number of pleats. This will give you the width of each pleat (roughly 20 cm [8 in]).

5
As there is always one less space than pleats, subtract one from the proposed number of pleats.

6
Subtract the overlaps (2 x 5 cm [2 in]) from the required finished width of the curtain.

7
Divide the difference by the number of spaces. This will give you the width of each space.

EXAMPLE
1 Required finished width = 140 cm (55 in)
2 140 cm (55 in) x 2.5 for fullness = 350 cm (138 in)
3 350 cm (138 in) – 140 cm (55 in) = 210 cm (83 in)
4 210 cm (83 in) ÷ 11 = 19.1 cm (7½ in) per pleat
5 11 – 1 = 10 spaces
6 140 cm (55 in) – 10 cm (4 in) overlaps = 130 cm (51 in)
7 130 cm (51 in) ÷ 10 = 13 cm [5¼ in] per space

MARKING UP FRENCH PLEATS

With tailor's chalk, mark the spacing and stitchlines on the right side of the hemmed curtain. Make sure that each mark is made to the correct length of the pleat (that is, they should not extend below the width of the buckram/stiffening).

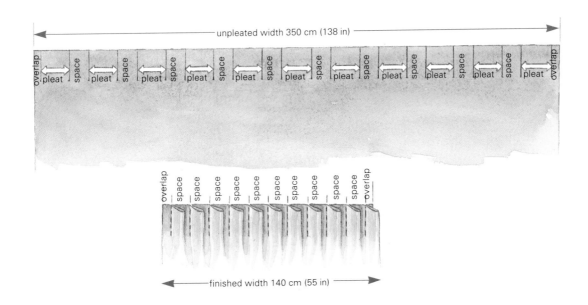

EQUIPMENT

f ind these items in department stores and in shops selling hardware, fabrics, haberdashery or craft materials.

1   standard (rufflette) tape
2   blind tape
3   plastic rings
4   cord pulls (toggles)
5   pencil-pleat tape
6   cleats
7   screw eyes
8   dowel rods
9   Velcro
10 elastic
11 retractable metal tape measure
12 blind cord
13 calico (for patterns)
14 iron-on interfacing
15 double-sided fusible bonding material
16 tracing paper (for patterns)
17 string
18 buttons
19 bases for covered buttons
20 hooks
21 curtain weights
22 calculator, pencil and notepaper
23 bias binding
24 readymade quilting fabric
25 piping
26 quick stitch unpicker
27 zips
28 pinhooks (for securing ends of curtains)
29 thimble
30 pins and needles
31 tailor's chalk
32 cotton thread
33 dressmaker's scissors
34 dressmaker's tape measure
35 steam iron
36 newspaper (for patterns)
37 lightweight cardboard (for templates)
38 curtain interlining

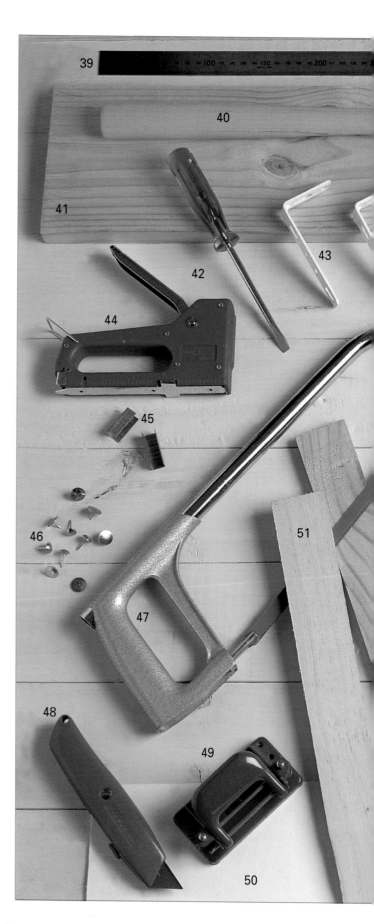

curtains

Window dressing IS A VERY IMPORTANT FEATURE IN A ROOM, SO TAKE THE TIME TO CHOOSE AN EFFECTIVE SCHEME. THE CHOICE IS UNLIMITED. FOR INSTANCE, LONG, FULL CURTAINS WILL COMPLEMENT A TRADITIONAL ROOM; SHEER CURTAINS WILL SCREEN THE WINDOW AND DIFFUSE THE LIGHT IN A MODERN ROOM; AND SHORT, CHINTZY CURTAINS WITH FRILLS WILL COMPLETE A COUNTRY COTTAGE LOOK. YOUR CURTAINS CAN ALSO BE USED TO 'PLAY' WITH THE PROPORTIONS OF THE WINDOWS, TO FRAME A PLEASANT OUTLOOK OR EVEN TO CAMOUFLAGE A BAD ONE. FABRIC SELECTION PLAYS A SIGNIFICANT ROLE, AND DULL OR PLAIN INTERIORS MAY BE ENLIVENED BY BRIGHTLY PATTERNED FABRICS. CHOOSE COLOUR CAREFULLY. BEAR IN MIND THAT THE LIGHT IN WHICH THE CURTAINS ARE DISPLAYED WILL ALTER THE COLOUR, AS WILL THE USE OF LINING. TEXTURE IN PLAIN FABRICS IS ANOTHER DIMENSION TO CONSIDER. IT ADDS INTEREST WITHOUT COMPLICATING THE COLOUR SCHEME, AND IS EMPHASIZED BY LIGHT FILTERING THROUGH THE CURTAINS.

OPPOSITE   This neutral colour-scheme is enriched by the textured curtain fabric and the elegant fringed valance.

MEASURING UP

decide on the look you want before measuring a window. Full-length curtains are more popular than short curtains because of their richer and more formal appearance. Short curtains are usually chosen for practical reasons, such as where cupboards or furniture restrict their length, and are therefore commonly used in kitchens and bathrooms.

As accuracy is crucial when measuring an opening for curtains, use a good retractable metal tape measure. Take your time and remember to check each measurement carefully. The more details you record, the better.

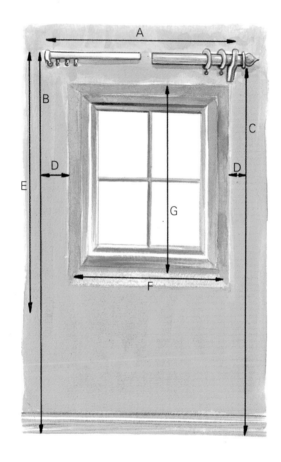

a Width of track or pole (rod), usually installed 10–20 cm (4–8 in) above the opening (the required finished width of the curtain/s is usually the same as this measurement)

b Finished length of a curtain which is to hang on a track, measured from the top of the track to the floor (once the tape and hooks are attached, the curtain will hang 1.5–2 cm (⅝–¾ in) above the floor)

c Finished length of a curtain which is to hang on a pole (rod) and rings, measured from the eye on the wooden ring to the floor

d Stacking space of the curtain, which varies according to the desired width of the window opening

e Finished length of short curtains, usually 10–15 cm (4–6 in) below the windowsill (unless obstructed by a cupboard or fixture of some sort)

f Width of inside window reveal (the required finished width of a blind may be the same as this measurement)

g Length of inside window reveal (the required finished length of a blind may be the same as this measurement)

To make a window look **wider**,
increase the stacking space.

To make a window look **taller**, install the fittings
higher than normal.

creating optical illusions

Add a deep pelmet to **disguise** an obvious gap
between the top of the window and the curtain fitting.

To make a window look **narrower**, join the curtains
in the centre and pull back with tiebacks.

To make a window look lower, add a deep pelmet, valance or swag.

To disguise different heights of openings in one room, install all the fittings at the same height.

ABOVE   The spaciousness of this tranquil sitting room is emphasized by the ceiling-height positioning of the window and door fittings.

WINDOW FITTINGS

isted below are some of the available window fitting options. Once you have chosen the style of curtain, you should decide on and install a suitable fitting and then take accurate measurements for your curtains (see page 24).

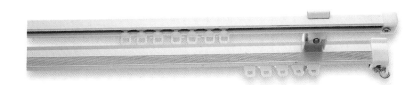

TRACKS

These are popular, economical and practical. Double and triple tracks can be used if a valance and/or voile curtain is required.

POLES AND RINGS

Available in all wood finishes, poles and rings can also be spray-painted white. Finials can be added.

WROUGHT-IRON RODS

These decorative fittings are available in a variety of designs, including those with or without rings.

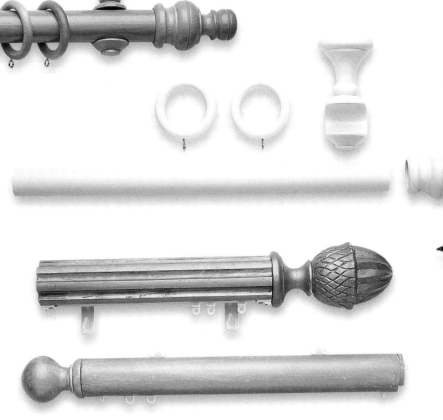

CONCEALED TRACK POLES

These fittings, also known as designer rods, disguise the track: the pole (which may have a diameter of 40 mm [1½ in], 50 mm [2 in] or 63 mm [2½ in]) is routed and a track and brackets are inserted inside the pole. Various finishes are available: natural and painted wood or brass, or they can even be covered in the curtain fabric. Finials can be added for extra effect.

CURTAIN HEADINGS

heading tapes

There are various heading tapes available. Each has a different effect, and some are more economical than others.

DEEP PINCH-PLEAT (KIRSCH) TAPE

This tape is gathered and held with four-pronged hooks. To calculate the amount of fabric you will need to accommodate the fullness of this curtain, multiply the width of the track or rod by 2.25. Deep pinch-pleat tape should be attached 1 cm (⅜ in) down from the top of the curtain. Four-pronged hooks have varying neck lengths, each of which is used with a different fitting: a short-necked hook is used with a track, while a long-necked hook is suitable for rod and rings. Adjustable hooks, which are very practical, are available.

PENCIL-PLEAT TAPE

This tape is gathered by pulling three strings to form narrow, vertical pleats, and is attached to the wall fitting with small plastic hooks. The fullness of the curtain is 2.5 to 2.75 times the width required. The tape should be attached 2 cm (¾ in) from the top of the curtain.

TWO-POCKET RUFFLETTE TAPE

Two-pocket rufflette tape has two strings and two pockets. The fullness of the curtain and positioning of the tape are the same as for standard tape.

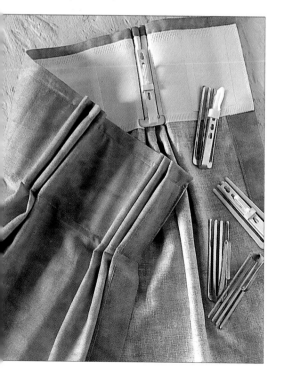

STANDARD (RUFFLETTE) TAPE

This narrow tape is pulled up with two strings to form soft gathers, and is attached to the wall fitting with small plastic hooks. The fullness of the curtain is 1.5 to 3 times the width required. Standard (rufflette) tape should be attached 3 cm (1¼ in) down from the top of the curtain.

heading variations

Apart from the conventional headings discussed opposite, there are more elaborate styles, such as French pleats, goblet pleats, and headings with ties, loops or eyelets. These are all made by hand without the use of special heading tapes.

FRENCH PLEATS

The appearance of this heading is similar to that of deep pinch-pleat (Kirsch) tape but, because it is folded by hand and each pleat is individually stitched, it shows a minimum amount of stitching on the right side of the fabric. French pleating must be stiffened with buckram (see glossary) or firm interfacing. The size and placing of the pleats must be carefully calculated so that the finished width of the curtain is correct. The fullness is 2.5 times that of the measured width, and the spacing of each pleat is usually 10–12 cm (4–4¾ in) apart. The first pleat should start about 5 cm (2 in) from the leading edge of the curtain, so that when the curtains are drawn closed they can overlap slightly. The length of the pleat may vary but should be no longer than the stiffening. A French pleat is not fixed at the top, but only down the back 'spine', and it is then machine or hand stitched across the base. The pleats splay open at the top as illustrated (fig 1). To calculate and mark up the pleats, refer to page 17.

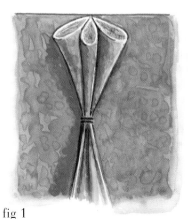

fig 1

1 Attach the stiffening to the top of the wrong side of the curtain. Pleat up, pushing the pleats forward to the right side of the curtain. Stitch down the back of the pleats (fig 2).

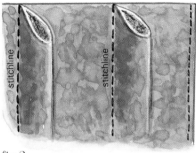

fig 2

2 Make three folds within the pleat, pressing the stiffening down firmly with your fingers (fig 3). Pin.

fig 3

3 Stitch across the base of the pleat, as illustrated above.

GOBLET PLEATS

These are similar to French pleats, except the main pleat is not folded but is shaped into a cap or tube and filled with wadding or curtain interlining. This filling is pushed well into the cup so that it is not visible once the curtain is hung. Proceed with steps 1 and 3 of French pleats but, after stitching across the base, round out the pleat with your fingers to form a goblet, as illustrated (fig 4). Fill the goblets with wadding or curtain interlining.

fig 4

HEADING WITH TIES OR LOOPS

This heading is very simple yet extremely effective and economical. Ties or loops are either sewn to the top of the curtain or inserted between the curtain and the lining and then stitched in place (fig 5). These ties or loops are hung directly onto a pole or tied through the rings on a pole – in this case, the curtain can be drawn easily.

fig 5

CALCULATING FABRIC QUANTITIES

for plain, striped and small-patterned fabrics

FORMULA

a   finished width x required fullness ÷ width of fabric = number of drops (lengths)

b   finished length + 25 cm (9¾ in) hem allowance x number of drops = quantity of fabric required

EXAMPLE 1 (METRIC)
Finished width = 200 cm
Finished length = 220 cm
Heading tape: deep pinch-pleat, therefore required fullness = x 2.25

a   200 cm x 2.25 ÷ 150 cm = 3 drops

b   220 cm + 25 cm x 3 = 7.35 m required

EXAMPLE 2 (METRIC)
Finished width = 250 cm
Finished length = 235 cm
Heading tape: pencil-pleat, therefore required fullness = x 2.5

a   250 cm x 2.5 ÷ 140 cm = 4.46 (rounded up) = 5 drops

b   235 cm + 25 cm x 5 = 13 m required

EXAMPLE 3 (IMPERIAL)
Finished width = 66 in
Finished length = 40 in
Heading tape: pencil-pleat, therefore required fullness = x 2.5

a   66 in x 2.5 ÷ 54 in = 3 drops

b   66 in + 10 in x 3 = 228 in = 6⅓ yd

EXAMPLE 4 (IMPERIAL)
Finished width = 72 in
Finished length = 80 in
Heading tape: deep pinch-pleat, therefore required fullness = x 2.25

a   72 in x 2.25 ÷ 48 in = 3.37 (rounded up) = 4 drops

b   80 in + 10 in x 4 = 360 in = 10 yd

for pattern-matching

If three drops of fabric are required for the full width of the window, the curtain on each side of the window will have one and a half drops, as shown in figure 6. The half drop must always be added on the outside of each curtain. If there is a large pattern on the fabric, each drop must be pattern-matched as shown in figure 7. Pattern-matching requires extra fabric (fig 8). The pattern repeat is usually indicated on the selvedge of the fabric or can be measured on the fabric.

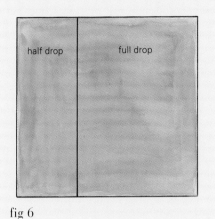

half drop · full drop

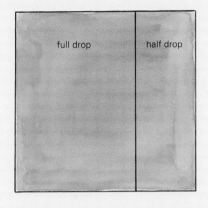

full drop · half drop

fig 6

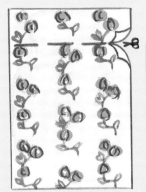

pattern repeat

fig 7

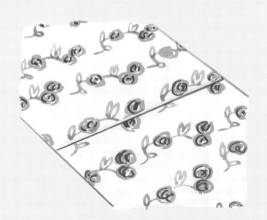

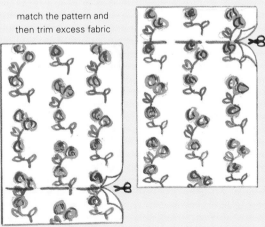

match the pattern and then trim excess fabric

fig 8

FORMULA

a   Finished length + 25 cm (10 in) hem allowance ÷ length of pattern = number of repeats (always round up to the nearest whole number)

b   Number of repeats x length of pattern = new cutting length

c   Number of drops x new cutting length = fabric required

EXAMPLE 1 (METRIC)
Finished length = 220 cm
Length of pattern = 64 cm

a   220 cm + 25 cm ÷ 64 cm = 3.82 = 4 repeats (rounded up)

b   4 x 64 cm = 256 cm (new cutting length)

c   3 x 256 cm = 7.68 m required

EXAMPLE 2 (IMPERIAL)
Finished length = 80 in
Length of pattern = 26 in

a   80 in + 10 in ÷ 26 in = 3.46 (rounded up) = 4 repeats

b   4 x 26 in = 104 in (new cutting length)

c   4 x 104 in = 416 in = 8¼ yd required

UNLINED CURTAINS

Unlined curtains are economical, very practical and, above all else, very easy to make. They are best used on windows where frequent washing may be necessary, such as kitchen and bathroom windows. Unlined curtains are a sensible choice for windows that do not receive a great deal of direct sunlight but where maximum light inside the room is still required. They provide privacy but do not block all the light. Detachable linings (see page 44) can always be attached at a later stage. Depending on the function of the curtain and the desired effect, the choice of headings and fittings is endless. Sheer and lightweight fabrics are well suited to the more decorative heading tapes.

gathered heading

1 Decide on the type of heading you wish to use, then calculate the amount of fabric required using the formula on page 30. If you need to match a pattern, calculate the fabric required for this using the formula on page 31.

2 Cut the required number of drops. Ensure that the cutting is straight, and cut off the selvedges to prevent puckering on the seams.

3 Join the drops using the seam of your choice (see page 9), and pattern-matching if necessary.

4 For the side hems, double-turn 3 cm (1¼ in). (The hems are double-turned to hide all raw edges.) The width of these hems may vary depending on the size of the curtain or the type of fabric used – shorter curtains and sheer fabrics should have narrower hems. Pin and tack in position. Press and stitch. If doing mitred corners (see pages 12–13), only stitch to within 15 cm (6 in) of the bottom hem foldline.

5 Fold the top 5 cm (2 in) of the curtain back to the wrong side, ensuring that all patterns line up. Press. Pin the heading tape in position on the

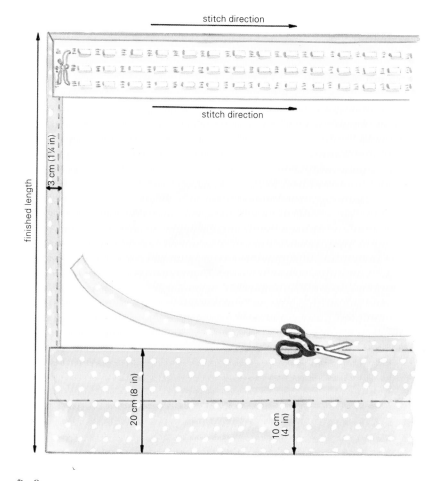

stitch direction

stitch direction

3 cm (1¼ in)

finished length

20 cm (8 in)

10 cm (4 in)

fig 9

wrong side of the curtain to cover the turned back raw edge. Fold the ends of the tape under and secure the cords if necessary. Avoiding the cords, stitch the

tape down carefully along the top and bottom, close to the edge and sewing both lines in the same direction to ensure that the tape stays flat (fig 9).

6 Lay the curtain flat on a large surface. Measure carefully from the top of the curtain to the required length and mark with pins. Then mark off the required hem allowance, measuring from the pins to the bottom of the fabric. A double-turned 10 cm (4 in) hem is standard (the hem allowance is therefore 20 cm [8 in]) but this may be narrower if the curtains are short or the fabric is extra-sheer. Trim off any excess fabric. Fold the hem towards the wrong side along the line of pins and press.

7 Full-length curtains usually require weights unless extra-sheer fabric is used. First cover the weights with a piece of lining or calico, as illustrated. Before stitching the bottom hem, insert and attach a weight into each corner and onto every seam (fig 10).

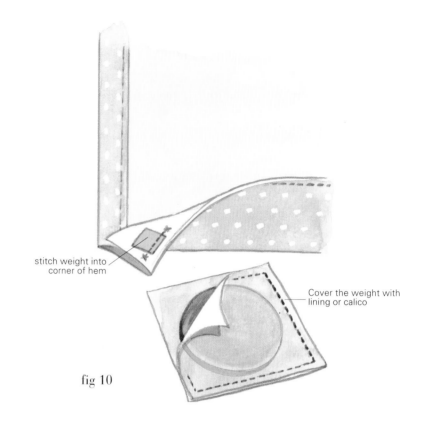

stitch weight into corner of hem

Cover the weight with lining or calico

fig 10

8 Double-turn the hem, press, pin and stitch, or, if mitring the corners, stitch to within 15 cm (6 in) of the side hem foldline.

9 Mitre the corners if required (see pages 12–13) – mitred corners work best where the side hems and the bottom hem are the same width.

10 Pull the cords of the heading tape to gather the curtain to the required width. Knot the ends. Spread the gathers evenly and insert the hooks.

IT IS BETTER TO ATTACH THE HEADING TAPE BEFORE STITCHING THE HEM SO THAT PATTERN-MATCHING CAN BE ACCURATE AT THE TOP WHERE IT IS MOST VISIBLE. SHOULD THE PATTERN RUN SLIGHTLY SKEW, THIS WILL BE LESS NOTICEABLE AT THE HEM.

▲

casing heading

This method is ideal for curtains that do not draw but remain permanently closed in the window or are held back with tiebacks. The size of the casing depends on the fittings chosen, for example, a wooden pole or metal rod, or stretch wire. Standard casing measurements are: 2 cm (¾ in) for stretch wire; 4 cm (1½ in) for a 16 mm (⅝ in) diameter rod or pole; and 7 cm (2¾ in) for a 38 mm (1½ in) diameter rod or pole. The heading may be enhanced by adding a frill above the casing.

When calculating the fabric quantities, you should take the width of the frill and casing into consideration. For example, 200 cm (79 in) required finished length + 20 cm (8 in) hem allowance + 5 cm (2 in) frill + 5 cm (2 in) back of frill + 7 cm (2¾ in) back of casing + 2 cm (¾ in) hem allowance = 239 cm (94½ in) cutting length.

1 Join the drops as for the unlined curtains with a gathered heading, stitching the side seams and hems and bottom hem as instructed on pages 32–34.

2 Lay the curtain flat on a large surface and measure the required length from the hem to the top of the frill. Fold all extra fabric at the top back towards the wrong side and press.

3 Working on the wrong side and from the top down, carefully measure the width of the frill and mark with pins – this will form the top of the casing. Measure the required length of the casing. Fold back the seam allowance and pin the bottom of the casing (fig 11). Tack in position then, sewing both rows in the same direction, stitch along the top and bottom of the casing, leaving the sides open.

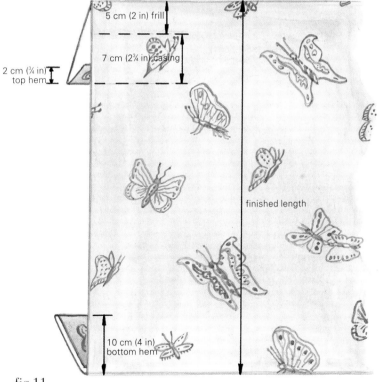

5 cm (2 in) frill

7 cm (2¾ in) casing

2 cm (¾ in) top hem

finished length

10 cm (4 in) bottom hem

fig 11

IF YOU ARE UNSURE OF THE CORRECT SIZE TO MAKE THE CASING, MEASURE THE CIRCUMFERENCE OF THE ROD, ADD 2 CM (¾ IN), AND THEN DIVIDE BY 2. FOR EXAMPLE, A 63 MM (2½ IN) ROD WILL HAVE A CIRCUMFERENCE OF 20 CM (8 IN) + 2 CM (¾ IN) ÷ 2 = 11 CM (4⅜ IN) CASING.

▲

CAFÉ CURTAINS

Café curtains provide privacy and can conceal unattractive views with minimum loss of light. They are often purely decorative and are usually installed inside the recess of the window. These curtains are mostly found in the kitchen although they may be adapted for the bathroom, or even doubled up with standard curtains in the bedroom where permanent privacy is required. The fabric used for café curtains may vary from extra sheer to lined cottons. Because of the wide choice of headings suitable for these curtains, they can be used to make an attractive feature of a window.

scalloped heading

A curtain with a scalloped heading usually hangs flat in the window, like the one described here, but can be made fuller with the addition of small pleats to the 'loops' between the scallops.

1. Referring to figure 12, make a template for the scallops using either a compass or a saucer with a diameter of 10 cm (4 in): draw a circle on firm paper or card. Draw a line AB through the centre of the circle. Draw perpindicular lines measuring 5 cm (2 in) from A to C and from B to D respectively. These vertical lines may be extended if deeper scallops are required. Join C to D so that CD equals AB. Cut out the template, which will be rounded at one end and flat at the other.

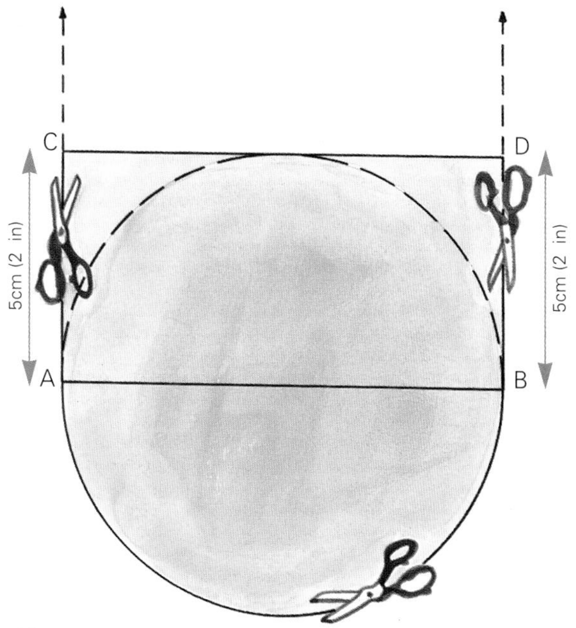

2. To calculate the cutting length for the curtain, add a 10 cm (4 in) hem allowance and 15 cm (6 in) for the back of the scallop (or more for a deeper scallop) to the required finished length of the curtain.

3. Join the drops of the curtain as instructed for unlined curtains on page 32.

4. Cut a strip of iron-on interfacing 13 cm (5¼ in) wide (or depth of scallop + 3 cm [1¼ in]) and 4–6 cm (1⅝–2¼ in) shorter than the full width of the curtain.

5. Iron the interfacing onto the wrong side of the curtain 1.5 cm (⅝ in) down from the top edge and 2–3 cm (¾–1¼ in) in from the side edges. Turn down the top 1.5 cm (⅝ in) of the curtain, press and stitch (fig 13).

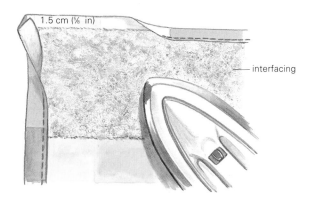

fig 12

fig 13

6 Double-turn 2–3 cm (¾–1¼ in) side hems, press and stitch.

7 Fold the interfaced top piece to the right side, pin down carefully and accurately (fig 14). Mark the top centre of the curtain. Centre the template on this mark and, holding it firmly in position, mark the scallop. Continue marking the scallops about 4–5 cm (1½–2 in) apart along the top of the curtain.

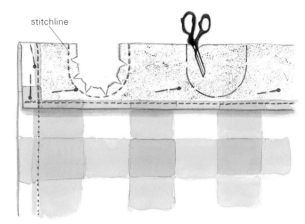

stitchline

fig 14

8 Stitch carefully along the marked lines. Trim and snip at intervals along the curved seams, as illustrated above.

9 Turn right side out and press carefully. Turn the facing in at the side hems and slipstitch closed (fig 15). If desired, the edges of the scallops may be topstitched.

topstitching (optional)

fig 15

ABOVE To make this pleated café curtain, allow extra fabric, space the scallops wider apart and form pleats between the scallops.

WHEN MARKING THE END OF THE SCALLOP PATTERN ON EACH SIDE OF THE CURTAIN IT IS BEST TO END IT JUST BEFORE AN INDIVIDUAL SCALLOP OR HALFWAY ACROSS ONE.

▲

10 Stitch rings, fabric loops or ties to the top of each scallop (fig16). Thread onto the pole in the window and mark the correct hemline.

fig 16

11 Double-turn a 5 cm (2 in) hem along this line and stitch.

looped heading

A curtain made with a looped heading is not gathered and therefore uses very little fabric, making it an economical option. It is ideal for a window that simply needs masking. To make the loops, merely extend the scallops to 20 cm (8 in) for a large loop, or 10 cm (4 in) for a smaller loop. Proceed as for scalloped heading, but instead of attaching rings, loops or ties, fold the fabric to the back, as illustrated (fig 17), pin and stitch.

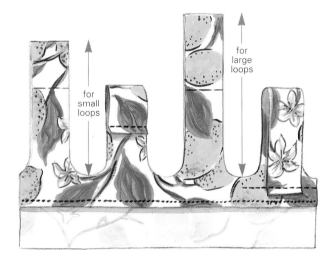

for large loops

for small loops

fig 17

ABOVE Here the curtain rod has been threaded through small loops for a simple yet attractive effect.

ruched heading

This casing heading is the best choice if sheer or lightweight fabric is to be used – other headings require more stable fabrics in order to achieve the best results. Sheer fabrics are too soft and transparent for elaborate headings to be successful. See page 35 for instructions for making a casing heading.

ABOVE An easy casing heading is ideal for lightweight fabrics.

LINED CURTAINS

any type of lining will protect a curtain. Linings increase insulation, warmth and darkness, and improve the fall of the curtain. They add body and weight to the curtain fabric and create a richer, more formal look. It is important that the lining should be compatible with the curtain fabric in terms of weight and colour. Heavyweight curtain fabrics need a thicker lining, whereas lightweight cottons may be lined with polyester. The colour of the lining should be chosen according to the colour of the curtain (a dark lining may ruin the appearance of a light curtain). The width of the lining fabric should also match that of the curtain fabric.

For all lined curtains, first join the curtain drops, pattern-matching if necessary, and ensuring that half drops are attached on the outside. Snip the selvedges at regular intervals to prevent puckering. Press the seams open.

Join the lining drops and press the seams open. There are many ways to attach the lining to the curtain, but we have chosen the three most popular; use any of the methods described on the following pages to attach the lining to the curtain.

linings

COTTON OR POLYESTER/COTTON

This lining is usually used for lightweight curtains that may need regular washing. It is also suitable for curtains in a window that does not receive harsh sunlight, or where privacy is needed without loss of natural light.

COTTON SATEEN

This is the most popular type of lining because it is substantially thicker and heavier than cotton or polyester/cotton lining. Cotton sateen is a stronger fabric with a shiny outer surface which helps to resist dust. It is advisable to buy pre-shrunk cotton sateen, which is available in various colours and shades.

BLOCK-OUT LINING

Block-out lining is a heavy fabric with a specialized finish on one side. It cuts out light completely and is very effec-tive in any room where total darkness is required during daylight hours. It may deaden the colours of a curtain by preventing natural light from shining through the fabric. Block-out lining may be sewn into the curtain or it may be detachable, if sewn with detachable-lining tape (see page 44). Detachable block-out lining is more practical when it comes to laundering the curtains.

INTERLINING

This is a thick, blanket-type lining with a fluffy, brushed-cotton feel, and it is positioned between the curtain and the normal lining, giving the curtain a luxurious, heavy appearance. It blocks out light and noise very effectively. However, it can deaden the appearance of the curtain, dulling the colours by preventing natural light from shining through. Flannelette may be used as an alternative to interlining.

> THE CUTTING LENGTH OF A LINING
> IS THE FINISHED LENGTH OF THE
> CURTAIN PLUS 15 CM (6 IN).
> ▲

sewn-in lining

Here the lining is placed under the prepared side hems of the curtain and sewn into place, enclosing the raw side edges. The lining is slipstitched by hand, unless otherwise instructed.

5   If interlining is required, prepare as for the lining, place under the lining and proceed as if they were one piece of fabric.

6   Lay the curtain flat on a large surface. With wrong sides facing and top edges aligned, place the lining on top of the curtain. The lining should lie about 2–3 cm (¾–1¼ in) shorter than the curtain.

7   Place the side edges of the lining beneath the folded side hems of the curtain (fig 18). Slipstitch the side seams closed, turning in the raw edges at the bottom of the hem, as illustrated.

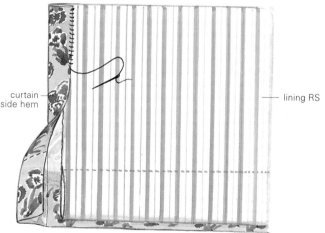

curtain side hem   lining RS

fig 18

1   Double-turn a 10 cm (4 in) bottom hem into the curtain, press and machine stitch.

2   Double-turn 3 cm (1¼ in) side hems into the curtain. Press but do not stitch.

3   Double-turn a 7 cm (2¾ in) bottom hem into the lining, press and stitch by machine.

4   Cut 3 cm (1¼ in) off each side edge of the lining.

8   Measure the required finished length of the curtain from the hem to the top. Mark with pins.

9   Fold the top over towards the wrong side along the marked line and press. Trim off any excess fabric.

10   Pin the heading tape in the correct position (see page 28). Stitch carefully, making sure that the trimmed and pressed top edge is enclosed by the tape.

11   Pull the tape up to the required width, securing the cords neatly.

loose lining

This lining is sewn in along the top of the curtain but attached with thread loops down the side hems. This is the most popular and practical lining, allowing for movement such as shrinkage or the dropping of the fabric without ruining the appearance of the curtain. The lining may be stitched by machine or slipstitched by hand.

1 Double-turn 3 cm (1¼ in) side hems and a 10 cm (4 in) bottom hem into the curtain. Press.

2 If the curtain requires weights, insert them into the hem (see page 34). Stitch the hem.

3 Double-turn 3 cm (1¼ in) side hems and a 7 cm (2¾ in) bottom hem into the lining, press and stitch.

4 Lay the curtain flat on a large surface and measure the required finished length from the hem to the top of the curtain. Mark with pins.

5 Fold the top of the curtain over towards the wrong side along this marked line. Press. This top hem must be 3 cm (1¼ in) wide – measure, then trim any excess fabric.

6 Pin the heading tape in the correct position, and stitch along the top of the tape only.

7 Lay the curtain flat on a large surface. With wrong sides together, place the lining on top of the curtain.

8 Place the top edge of the lining beneath the heading tape, trimming off any excess. The lining must lie flush against the top row of stitching, and should be about 2–3 cm (¾–1¼ in) shorter than the curtain (fig 19).

9 If interlining is required, prepare as for the lining and sandwich the interlining between the curtain and the lining.

10 Carefully pin along the lower edge of the heading tape, enclosing the top edge of the lining. Stitch along this pinned line as well as down the sides of the tape, taking care not to catch the cords.

11 Sew the lining to the curtain along the side hems by making 3 cm (1¼ in) loops at regular intervals. To make the thread loops, first make a large stitch from the lining to the curtain. (If the curtain is interlined, the loop should catch the curtain, the interlining and the lining.) Then make blanket stitches along the length of the loop (fig 20). Firmly secure the end of the loop.

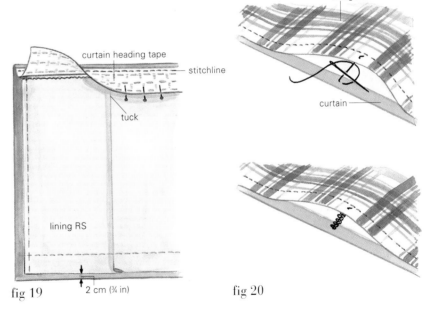

curtain heading tape — stitchline

tuck

lining RS

fig 19   2 cm (¾ in)

lining RS

curtain

fig 20

IF THE LINING IS SLIGHTLY WIDER THAN THE CURTAIN, TAKE THE EXTRA FABRIC IN WITH LITTLE TUCKS MADE IN THE LINING ALONG THE TOP (AS ILLUSTRATED IN FIG 19). ONCE THE CURTAIN IS GATHERED AND HANGING, THESE TUCKS WILL BE CONCEALED.

▲

detachable lining

Although this lining is hung from the same hooks as the curtain, it is made completely separately from the curtain and has its own heading tape called detachable-lining tape. This tape is stitched over the top edge of the lining and has slits through which the curtain hooks are pushed (see below). To economize, these linings need not be as full as the curtains. The stitching may be done by machine or slipstitched by hand, unless otherwise instructed. Make and hang the curtain as instructed for unlined curtains on pages 32–34. Note that the detachable lining is made 10 cm (4 in) shorter than the curtain.

1 Double-turn 3 cm (1¼ in) side hems and a 7 cm (2¾ in) bottom hem into the lining. Press and stitch.

2 Lay the lining flat on a large surface and measure the finished length from the hem to the top. Mark with pins.

3 Trim the lining along this marked line. Place the lining heading tape over the top edge of the lining, leaving extra tape at the sides for turning in (fig 21). Stitch along the bottom edges of the tape, enclosing the raw edge of the lining and turning back the sides of the tape.

4 Gather the tape up to the required width. Thread the curtain hooks through the appropriate slits in the lining tape, and then attach them to the curtain heading tape (the lining and curtain thus share the same hooks).

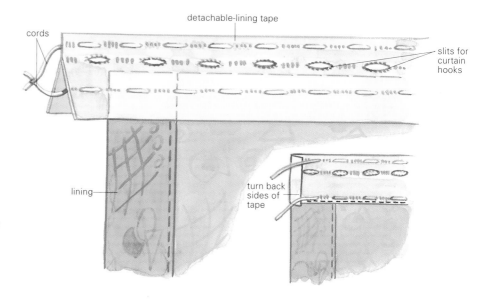

fig 21

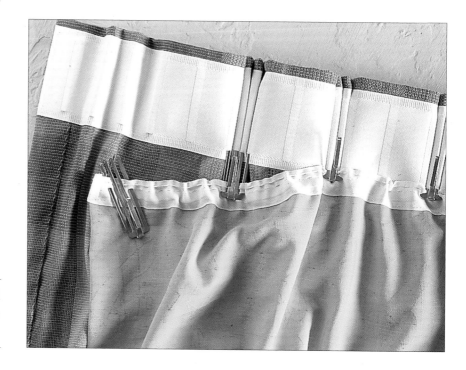

RIGHT The curtain hooks are threaded through the detachable-lining tape before being hooked into the curtain tape.

BORDERS AND TRIMS

a contrast border, fringing, lace, frill, ribbon or binding can transform the simplest of curtains, valances or blinds. The size of the trim should be considered in relation to the length of the curtain and the size of the window. Borders and trims may be added after the curtain has been completed, however it is preferable to attach them during the initial construction of the curtain. Should a flat border be made with fabric, ensure that it is compatible with the curtain fabric to prevent puckering. See Sewing Techniques (pages 8–17) for further information and ideas.

HOLDBACKS AND TIEBACKS

tiebacks or holdbacks do exactly that: they tie or hold the curtain back, either for practical reasons or purely to be decorative. They enable one to transform a simply dressed window into an attractive feature, with the gracefully draped curtain softening any harsh lines. In addition, by holding the curtain back the maximum amount of light is able to penetrate the window, and, in a doorway, the held-back curtain does not become a hindrance.

HOLDBACKS

a holdback may be in the form of either a knob or an arm which embraces the curtain. They can only hold back a limited amount of fabric. Because holdbacks are mounted on the wall, they draw the curtain back beyond the reveal of the window. Choose a holdback which coordinates with the décor of your room as well as with the curtain fitting and fabric used.

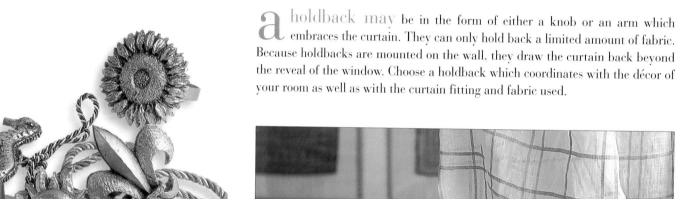

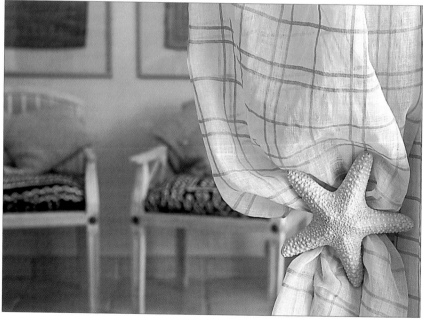

TO ASSIST WITH DRAPING AND RETAINING THE ELEGANT FOLDS OF A NEWLY HUNG CURTAIN,
LET THE CURTAIN FALL NATURALLY, THEN PLEAT THESE NATURAL FOLDS AND
TIE THE CURTAIN BACK FIRMLY FOR AT LEAST TWO DAYS.

TIEBACKS

tiebacks are usually positioned about 1 metre (3 ft 3 in) above floor level. However, if there are features at the curtained opening which draw the eye, such as window sills, it is aesthetically more pleasing to line up the tiebacks with these. Be sure to secure the wall hooks or fixtures carefully, as they often need to support a fairly heavy weight.

crescent-shaped tieback

This popular tieback is the most conventional one used, and the broad shape holds the curtain without crushing the fabric. To calculate the correct length of the tieback, measure around the hanging curtain as illustrated (fig 22).

1 m (3 ft 3 in)

fig 22

USEFUL GUIDE TO CALCULATING REQUIREMENTS FOR TIEBACKS			
METRIC			
No. of drops	Length of tieback	Req. fabric/pair	Req. piping/pair
1	55–60 cm	40 cm	3 m
1½ to 2	75–80 cm	50 cm	3.8 m
2½ to 3	85–100 cm	80 cm	4.25 m
3½ to 4	120–140 cm	90–100 cm	6 m
IMPERIAL			
No. of drops	Length of tieback	Req. fabric/pair	Req. piping/pair
1	22–24 in	16 in	3¼ yd
1½ to 2	30–31 in	20 in	4 yd
2½ to 3	33–39 in	31 in	4¼ yd
3½ to 4	47–55 in	36–39 in	6½ yd

plaited tieback

PROJECT REQUIREMENTS

Fabric for each 'sausage'
Wadding or interlining for the filling
2 curtain rings per tieback

1 Calculate the required length of the tieback as illustrated on page 49, but add half the length again to allow extra fabric for the plaiting.

2 The size or thickness of the 'sausages' may vary according to the desired effect. The standard size is made from 15–20 cm (6–8 in) wide fabric strips. Cut three strips for each tieback.

3 Cut equivalent strips of wadding or interlining for each 'sausage'. Tack the wadding or interlining to the wrong side of each strip of fabric.

4 With the right sides together, fold each strip in half lengthwise. Stitch lengthwise along the edge (fig 27.1) and then turn right side out as illustrated (fig 27.2). Centre the seam on the underside of each 'sausage'.

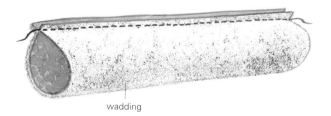

wadding

fig 27.1

centre the seam

fig 27.2

5 Place the top edges of the three 'sausages' together. Double-turn the raw edges, and stitch together firmly, as illustrated (fig 28).

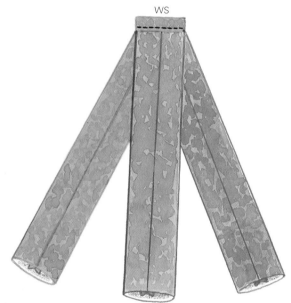

WS

fig 28

6 Plait the 'sausages', ensuring that the centre-back seams always face the underside of the tieback.

7 Check the length of the tieback, trimming if necessary before securing the three ends of the plait. Double-turn the raw edges and stitch firmly. Attach a curtain ring to each end of the tieback (fig 29).

fig 29

SHOULD THE TIEBACK BE A BIT SHORT, ATTACH A HEMMED STRIP OF FABRIC TO THE END OF THE TIEBACK THEREBY BRINGING IT TO THE CORRECT LENGTH. THIS STRIP WILL HANG OUT OF SIGHT BEHIND THE CURTAIN.

FOR A ROPELIKE EFFECT, USE TWO 'SAUSAGES' INSTEAD OF THREE AND TWIST THEM TOGETHER.
ALTERNATIVELY, USE TWO 'SAUSAGES' AND MAKE A KNOT IN THE CENTRE.

CHAPTER

pelmets
and
curtain valances

Pelmets and valances ARE PLACED ABOVE WINDOWS, ADDING A FINISHED LOOK TO THE TOP OF THE WINDOW, COVERING AND CAMOUFLAGING THE TRACK AND COMPLETING THE 'FRAMING' OF THE OPENING. THEY CAN ALSO BE USED TO CREATE A CLEVER ILLUSION OF HEIGHT: BY INSTALLING THE PELMET OR VALANCE HIGHER THAN THE TRACK THE HEIGHT OF THE CURTAIN CAN BE DISGUISED AND THE PROPORTIONS OF THE WINDOW ALTERED. IN ADDITION, THEY PROTECT THE CURTAIN FROM DUST AND DIRT. A VALANCE USUALLY GIVES A SOFT, DRAPED EFFECT, WITH THE GATHERED OR PLEATED FABRIC ATTACHED TO A DOUBLE OR TRIPLE TRACK, OR TO A PELMET SHELF. PELMETS ARE FIRM AND THUS MORE FORMAL THAN VALANCES. USUALLY THEY ARE UPHOLSTERED AND FITTED EITHER TO A PELMET SHELF OR TO A COMPLETE PELMET BOX FOR EXTRA SUPPORT. THERE ARE ANY NUMBER OF ATTRACTIVE STYLES TO CHOOSE FROM, BUT BE SURE TO MAINTAIN BALANCE AND PROPORTION WHEN MAKING YOUR SELECTION.

OPPOSITE   A box-pleated valance is trimmed with heavy bullion fringing to emphasize the soft folds and the richness of the curtain fabric.

PELMETS

the depth of the pelmet should not, as a general rule, exceed one-sixth of the full length of the curtain, however this will depend on the individual window and the appearance desired. A pelmet is firm and should be mounted onto a box or shelf (topboard). The shape of the pelmet should also suit the style of the room, the window and the chosen fabric. Buckram is an adequate stiffener for the façade of most pelmets, but a wooden base is necessary for large-scale pelmets and in rooms where

moist air could warp the buckram. Hardboard is also suitable. Decide on the required shape and length of the pelmet. Cut a paper template to this shape, measuring the full width of the pelmet shelf (topboard) plus any returns; the depth of the template is equal to the required depth of the finished pelmet. Mark the centre of the pelmet on the template and cut the buckram or wooden façade to fit the template.

There are three different designs of pelmet shelf (topboard), shown below, to which the pelmet can be attached.

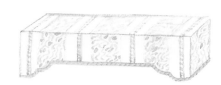

BASIC PELMET SHELF

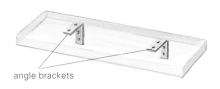

angle brackets

The shelf is usually made from a piece of wood which is 2 cm (¾ in) thick, the same length as the track above which it is to be fitted, and 10 cm (4 in) wide. This width leaves enough clearance for the curtains to run unobstructed on a track below. Should there be a double track, a wider pelmet shelf is necessary. The pelmet is attached to the pelmet shelf with Velcro, panel pins or staples.

PELMET SHELF WITH WOODEN RETURNS

The returns, placed vertically on each side of the pelmet shelf, give extra support to the pelmet, which may thus be heavier and deeper in design than a pelmet used with a pelmet shelf only.

COMPLETE PELMET BOX

This consists of a pelmet shelf, returns and façade, and is used for a fully upholstered pelmet or a heavy one needing solid support. The façade is made from wood, although plywood or hardboard may be used (but, as the function of a complete box is to provide more support than the other shelves, the material should not be too lightweight). Shape the façade with a jigsaw.

simple upholstered pelmet

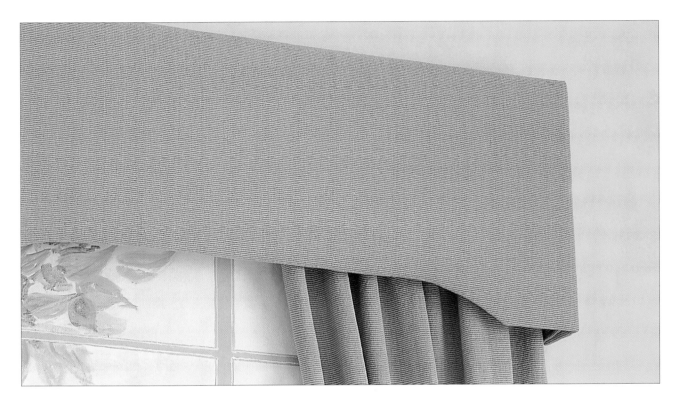

PROJECT REQUIREMENTS

Complete pelmet box
Fabric cut to the size of the template plus
5 cm (2 in) hem allowance all round
Interlining or thin foam cut to the size of the pelmet plus
3 cm (1¼ in) hem allowance all round

Lining cut to the size of the template plus
1.5 cm (⅝ in) hem allowance all round
Staple gun and staples
Glue
Piping if required

1 Glue the interlining or foam to the front and returns of the pelmet box. Snip any curves. Fold the hem allowance to the back and glue, being sure to keep a neat, flat edge, as illustrated (fig 1).

2 Place the fabric in position, centring any large patterns. Fold back the hem allowance (this will be about 2 cm [¾ in]; the rest of the hem allowance is absorbed by the fullness of the interlining or foam). Staple the fabric to the top of the pelmet box, working from the centre out towards the sides (fig 2). Repeat this process along the bottom edge, snipping any curves.

3 If piping is required, handstitch it along the inside of the bottom edge of the pelmet.

4 The lining is placed right side up on the inside of the pelmet. Fold the 1.5 cm (⅝ in) hem allowance under towards the inside. Staple in position, enclosing all raw edges (fig 3).

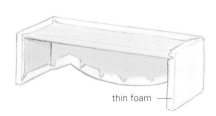

thin foam

fig 1

fig 2

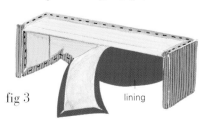

fig 3

lining

CURTAIN VALANCES

a valance is a deep fabric heading placed above the curtain. Gathered valances have a softer, less formal appearance than that of box-pleated or flat valances. The depth of the valance will depend on the style chosen but, generally, should not exceed one-sixth of the length of the curtain. There are two suitable fittings to which a valance can be attached, namely a double or triple track, or a pelmet shelf with either Velcro or curtain heading tape attached to it.

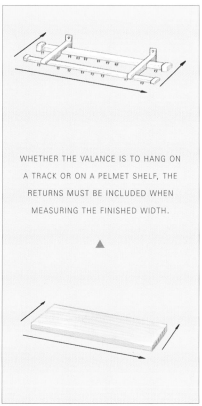

WHETHER THE VALANCE IS TO HANG ON A TRACK OR ON A PELMET SHELF, THE RETURNS MUST BE INCLUDED WHEN MEASURING THE FINISHED WIDTH.

LEFT The gently curving lines of this gathered valance are emphasized by the piped frill along the top, and the thick bullion fringing which trims the bottom.

lined, gathered valance

Decide on the depth of the valance. Depending on the choice of heading, calculate the fullness and the required number of drops, as instructed on page 30. Add 15 cm (6 in) for the hems. If the fabric has a pattern repeat, calculate the fabric according to the formula on page 31. If the valance is unlined, follow the instructions given for unlined curtains on page 32, except the valance hem should be only 5 cm (2 in) wide, double-turned.

ADDITIONAL PROJECT REQUIREMENTS

Heading tape of your choice
Curtain hooks or Velcro

1 Cut the lining drops 7 cm (2¾ in) shorter than the valance drops.

2 Join the valance drops, pattern-matching if necessary, and press. Join the lining drops and press.

3 Lay the valance flat on a large surface. With right sides together and bottom edges aligned, lay the lining on top of the fabric, matching any joins.

4 Pin and stitch the bottom edge of the valance and lining, using a 1.5 cm (⅝ in) seam allowance. Press.

5 Turn to the right side. Fold back the lining plus the bottom 8 cm (3⅛ in) of the valance to form the hem, as illustrated (fig 4).

6 Double-turn the lining and the fabric together to make 3 cm (1¼ in) side hems and stitch.

7 Measure the correct finished length of the valance from the hem to the top, and mark with pins. Fold the top of the fabric and lining towards the wrong side along the marked line, and press. Trim any excess fabric.

8 Attach the chosen heading tape in the correct position, as instructed on page 28, and stitch.

9 Should the valance be attached to a track, pull the cords up to the required width and insert the hooks.

10 Should the valance be attached with Velcro to a pelmet shelf, first attach the heading tape and then stitch the soft Velcro onto the tape as illustrated (fig 5), being careful not to stitch over the cords. Pull the cords up to the required width.

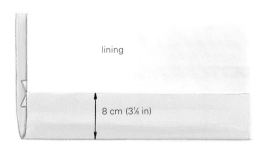

lining

8 cm (3⅛ in)

fig 4

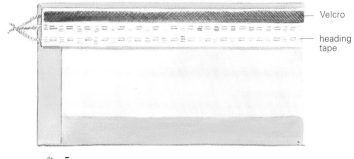

Velcro

heading tape

fig 5

box-pleated valance

A box-pleated valance is more formal than the gathered valance and uses fabric quite extravagantly. Velcro is used to attach the valance to the pelmet shelf.

ADDITIONAL PROJECT REQUIREMENTS

Lining if using
Velcro, or facing/tape and drawing pins or staples

1 The fullness required for this valance is three times that of the finished width.

2 Cut the number of drops required and join, pattern-matching if necessary (see page 31).

3 If the valance is to be unlined, double-turn a 5 cm (2 in) hem, press and stitch.

4 If the valance is to be lined, join the lining drops and attach as instructed on page 59, steps 3–5.

5 Double-turn 3 cm (1¼ in) side hems, press and stitch.

6 Measure the correct length of the valance from the hem to the top, and mark with pins. Fold the fabric to the wrong side along this marked line and press well. Trim any excess fabric.

7 Calculate the size of the pleats making sure that they are evenly distributed, and marking the pleats and

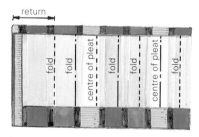

fig 6

spaces on the wrong side, as illustrated (fig 6). The size and spacing of the pleats may vary depending on the chosen style.

8 Pin the pleats securely in position, keeping the top of the valance straight (fig 7). Tack the pleats if necessary. Check that the width of the valance fits the pelmet shelf correctly.

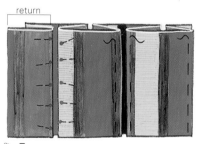

fig 7

9 Pin soft Velcro to the top of the valance on the wrong side, as illustrated (fig 8). Stitch neatly and straight along the top, being careful not to disarrange the pleats. Stitch along the

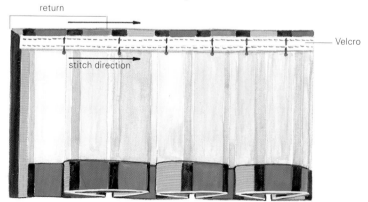

fig 8

bottom of the Velcro in the same direction, enclosing all raw edges.

10 Glue or staple the coarse Velcro to the pelmet shelf, and attach the valance to this.

11 As an alternative to Velcro, stitch a 'facing' or 'tape' to the top of the valance and attach to the top of the pelmet shelf with drawing pins or staples, as illustrated (fig 9)

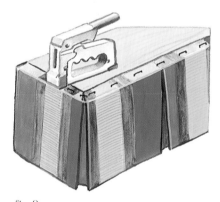

fig 9

economical box-pleated valance

This valance is not at all fussy and uses minimal fabric. The pleats are made on the corners of the pelmet shelf only, as illustrated (fig 10). A centre pleat is optional and is usually added to very wide windows. Allow approximately 40 cm (16 in) for each pleat.

fig 10

CHAPTER three

swags and tails

Swags and tails MAY BE USED TO GREAT EFFECT AROUND WINDOWS OR DOORS. WHILE THEY CAN BE USED ON THEIR OWN OR TO ENHANCE A ROMAN BLIND, SWAGS AND TAILS ARE BEST COUPLED WITH FULL-LENGTH CURTAINS. FOR STANDARD OPENINGS SINGLE SWAGS ARE USED, BUT IF THE OPENING IS VERY WIDE MULTIPLE SWAGS, USUALLY OVERLAPPING ONE ANOTHER, ARE MORE PRACTICAL. EACH SWAG IS MADE SEPARATELY AND SHOULD BE GENEROUS AND FULL. TAILS, TOO, ARE MADE SEPARATELY. THE STYLE OF THE TAILS MAY VARY BUT THEY SHOULD HANG A THIRD TO HALFWAY DOWN THE LENGTH OF THE CURTAIN. THEY MAY BE FORMALLY CONCERTINA-PLEATED OR MERELY GATHERED FOR AN INFORMAL EFFECT. THE SHAPE OF THE TAIL WILL AFFECT THE WAY THAT IT FALLS.

WHILE FORMAL SWAGS AND TAILS ARE TRADITIONALLY USED TO COMPLEMENT AN OPENING, A LESS FORMAL MODE OF SWAGGING IS BECOMING VERY POPULAR. INFORMAL SWAGGING USES A SINGLE PIECE OF FABRIC SHAPED TO CREATE ITS OWN SWAGS AND TAILS. THE LENGTH OF THIS FABRIC WILL DETERMINE THE FULLNESS AND STYLE OF THE DRAPE. THE FABRIC FOR SWAGS AND TAILS SHOULD BE SELECTED WITH CARE TO ENSURE THAT IT HAS A NATURAL TENDENCY TO DRAPE WELL.

OPPOSITE   This formal window dressing, with its softly draped swags and tails, enhances the gracious character of the room.

four

blinds

blinds are an economical WAY OF SCREENING A WINDOW SIMPLY BECAUSE THEY USE MUCH LESS FABRIC THAN CURTAINS. WHILE BLINDS OFFER A RANGE OF STYLISH AND VERSATILE WINDOW TREATMENTS, FROM PLAIN TO EXOTIC, THEY ARE, ON THE WHOLE, CHOSEN FOR THEIR PRACTICAL ADVANTAGES: THEY USE RELATIVELY LITTLE FABRIC, NEED NOT OBSTRUCT THE WINDOW AREA AND ARE EASY TO OPERATE. THE SOFTLY SCALLOPED AND RUCHED EFFECT OF A FESTOON BLIND ADDS A FEMININE TOUCH AND A SUMPTUOUS ELEGANCE TO ANY ROOM. ON THE OTHER HAND, ROMAN BLINDS, WHICH HAVE BECOME VERY POPULAR OF LATE, HAVE A NEAT, GRAPHIC EFFECT AND ARE EXCEPTIONALLY USEFUL FOR GIVING A CRISP, MODERN LOOK TO CURVED BAY WINDOWS. NOTE THAT THE UTMOST ACCURACY MUST BE EXERCISED WHEN TAKING MEASURE-MENTS, MAKING UP AND STITCHING THE BLINDS, AS THE SMALLEST ERROR MAY INTER-FERE WITH THE WAY THEY WORK. IT IS ALSO IMPERATIVE TO FOLLOW THE INSTRUCTIONS CLOSELY FOR A SUCCESSFUL RESULT.

OPPOSITE   A mock box-pleated blind is combined with a roller blind for an effect which is both practical and visually pleasing.

ROMAN BLINDS

The beauty of a Roman blind lies in its simple, tailored appearance. When raised, the pleated folds lie neatly on top of one another, resembling a soft, layered pelmet. When let down, this blind is flat and uncluttered. Roman blinds are often attached inside the window reveal and may be used together with permanently held-back curtains or decorative swags and tails for added impact. The neat folding of the blind allows the maximum of light in, and works well in a sash window with an attractive architrave which frames both the blind and the window.

The secret of a successful Roman blind is knowing how to calculate the measurements of the different pockets (that is, the distance between the casings), so that the blind draws up evenly. The lining is very important as all the work is done on this rather than on the blind fabric, which is added later to the accurately measured and stitched lining. Before beginning any work, you should first measure the window carefully (see page 24) and establish the required finished length and width of the blind.

80

F O R M U L A

FOR CALCULATING THE POCKETS AND MARKING UP THE LINING

Follow these steps carefully in order to calculate the spacing of the pockets and dowel casings. (Note that the instructions for cutting the fabric and making up the blind are given on pages 84–87.) These measurements are marked on the lining of the blind, and all work should be done from the bottom of the blind up. With reference to figure 8 below, note that a Roman blind is always divided into an odd number of sections. A useful guideline is that a small blind may have 5 sections, a medium one 7–9 sections and a large one 11 or more. Each section must be between 12.5 cm (5 in) and 17.5 cm (7 in) long.

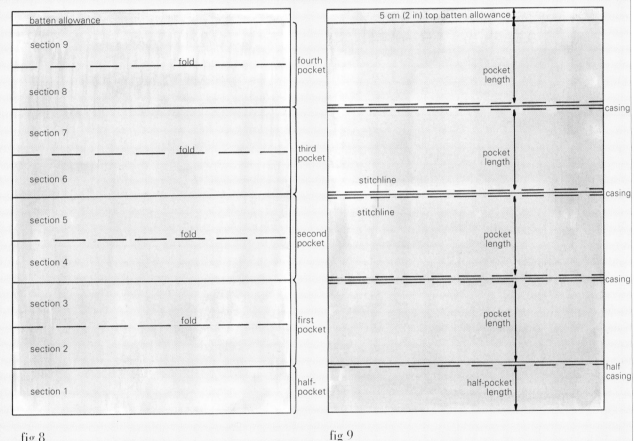

fig 8   fig 9

1 Subtract 5 cm (2 in) for the top batten allowance from the required finished length of the blind.

2 To calculate the size of each section, divide the rest of the blind measurement by an odd number until you get a figure between 12.5 cm (5 in) and 17.5 cm (7 in). The odd number will give you the number of sections your blind must have, and the figure between 12.5 cm (5 in) and 17.5 cm (7 in) will be the length of each section (note that each section will therefore be exactly the same size).

3 Each pocket is formed by two sections added together (the mid-line will form the foldline when the blind is pulled up). The bottom section is half the length of a pocket.

4 To allow for the dowel casings add 1.5 cm (⅝ in) to the bottom section and 3 cm (1¼ in) to each pocket (fig 9).

81

EXAMPLE OF A MEDIUM-LENGTH BLIND (METRIC)

Finished length of blind	= 140 cm
Subtract 5 cm for top batten	= 135 cm
Divide by 9 sections	= 15 cm/section
Therefore the bottom section	= 15 cm
Double this measurement	= 30 cm/pocket
Add 3 cm for the casing	= 33 cm
Multiply by number of full-sized pockets	
	= 4 x 33 cm
	= 132 cm
Add half-sized pocket and half-sized casing	
+ 15 cm + 1.5 cm = 148.5 cm	

To check whether the formula calculations are correct, add together all the measurements except those of the casings and bottom dowel. The total should equal that of your measured required finished length.

4 pockets x 30 cm	= 120 cm
+ Bottom section	= 15 cm
+ Top batten allowance	= 5 cm
Total	= 140 cm

EXAMPLE OF A LONG BLIND (IMPERIAL)

Finished length of blind	= 77½ in
Subtract 2 in for top batten	= 75½ in
Divide by 11 sections	= 6⅞ in, rounded off
	= 7 in/section
Therefore the bottom section	= 7 in
Double this measurement	= 14 in/pocket
Add 1¼ in for the casing	= 15¼ in
Multiply by number of full-sized pockets	
	= 5 x 15¼ in
	= 76¼ in
Add half-sized pocket and half-sized casing	
+ 7 in + ⅝ in = 83⅞ in	

To check whether the formula calculations are correct, add together all the measurements except those of the casings and bottom dowel. The total should equal that of your measured required finished length.

5 pockets x 14 in	= 70 in
+ Bottom section	= 7 in
+ Top batten allowance	= 2 in
Total	= 79 in

(The slight discrepancy in the calculation is negligible as this will be automatically eliminated when the blind is made up.)

ABOVE To make an unstructured Roman blind do not stitch casings. Instead attach the small plastic rings to the outer edges of the blind at regular intervals and insert a flat batten into the bottom hem. Thread the cords as you would a normal Roman blind. Lining is optional.

14 Repeat step 13, working from the bottom casing up to the top one, and constantly checking your accuracy.

15 Lay the blind flat and measure the required finished length from the bottom edge to the top. Mark with pins. Fold the fabric and lining to the wrong side along this line.

16 Leaving a 2 cm (¾ in) top hem allowance, trim the excess fabric and press.

17 Stitch soft Velcro to the top of the blind, enclosing the raw edges (fig 13). First stitch the top edge of the Velcro and then the bottom edge, sewing both in the same direction to prevent puckering.

18 Insert the flat batten into the bottom seam and slipstitch the side openings closed.

19 Cut the dowel rods to the same length as the dowel casings. Insert the rods into the casings. Slipstitch the casings closed.

20 Lay the blind flat on a large surface with the lining facing upwards. Measure and mark the positions of the rings on the casings. The first and last vertical rows of rings should be 10 cm (4 in) in from the side edges of the blind. The remaining vertical rows should be evenly distributed at approximately 30 cm (12 in) intervals along the width of the blind (fig 14). Stitch all the rings securely in place.

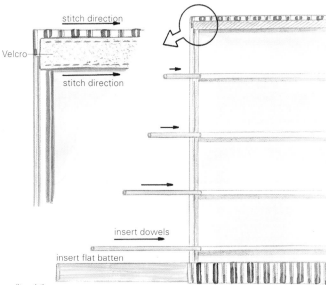

fig 13

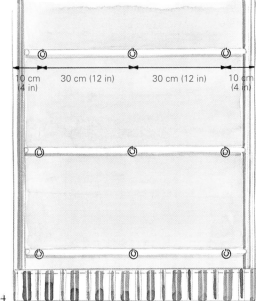

fig 14

21 Cut the top batten to the finished width of the blind.

22 Cover and prepare the batten as instructed for the festoon blind on page 76, steps 14 and 15, but note that the coarse Velcro should be attached to the front of the batten only and not down the sides.

23 Attach the blind to the batten by pressing the Velcro strips together.

24 Tie the cord securely to the bottom ring of the first vertical row, thread up through the remaining rings and then through the screw eyes in the batten to the side of the blind where the drawcords will be situated. Repeat, threading each vertical row of rings (fig 15).

25 Pull all the cords simultaneously, raising the blind. Check that the folds are even and straight.

26 Release the blind, firmly holding the cords together. Knot the cord about 50 cm (20 in) from the ends, then attach a cord pull to the loose ends.

27 Pull back the sides of the blind from the batten as far as the pilot holes (there is no need to remove the entire blind from the batten). Mount the batten to the wall or window frame through the pilot holes, and re-attach the sides of the blind.

28 Install a cleat on the wall or window frame on the same side as the drawcords, so that the cords can be secured when the blind is pulled up.

ABOVE The flat border around the edges of this Roman blind adds an elegant finish to an otherwise plain window treatment.

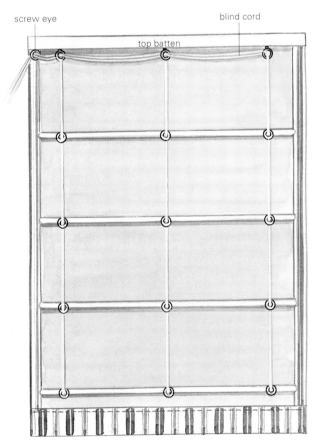

screw eye

blind cord

top batten

fig 15

cushions

the simplest way TO UPDATE OR COMPLETELY TRANSFORM YOUR DECORATING SCHEME IS TO ADD TO OR CHANGE THE CUSHIONS. CUSHIONS ALLOW YOU TO INTRODUCE COLOUR, PATTERN, TEXTURE, COMFORT AND STYLE. BE SURE TO CHOOSE A FILLING SUITABLE TO THE END PURPOSE OF THE CUSHION; FOR EXAMPLE, USE A THICK FOAM PAD FOR A BOX CUSHION WHICH WILL BE USED ON A HARD OR SLIGHTLY UNCOMFORTABLE SURFACE, OR SOFT AND YIELDING DOWN OR FEATHERS FOR A SCATTER CUSHION ON AN ARMCHAIR.

EVEN A SIMPLY STYLED CUSHION CAN BE DECORATED WITH INNUMERABLE TRIMS AND ACCESSORIES: USE BRAIDS, BORDERS, PIPING CORDS, TASSLES, BUTTONS, APPLIQUÉ, LACE, RIBBON OR FRINGING – THE CHOICE IS YOURS. A CUSHION MAY BE MADE INTO ANY SHAPE AND THE BASIC METHOD OF CONSTRUC-TION EASILY ADAPTED TO THE CHOSEN STYLE. CONSIDER THE END USE OF THE CUSHION WHEN SELECTING THE COVER FABRIC YOU ARE GOING TO USE: WASHABLE FABRICS AND TRIMS ARE ESSENTIAL FOR WELL-USED CUSHIONS.

OPPOSITE   Combine different fabrics and finishes such as piping, fringing, ties and Oxford-flaps for a never-ending variety of cushions.

side opening cushion with ties or buttons

1 Establish the size of the cushion. Cut the front and back pieces, adding a 1.5 cm (⅝ in) seam allowance all around.

2 Cut two extra pieces for the facings. These must be 10 cm (4 in) wide and the same length as the sides of the front and back pieces which will form the opening. Hem along the length on one side of each facing (fig 5).

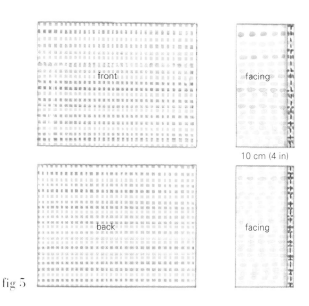

10 cm (4 in)

fig 5

3 Should piping be required, stitch it onto the right side of the cushion front (see page 12). Snip the corners.

4 If the cushion is to be closed with ties or ribbons, attach them now:

a First pin the ties in position on the opening edges of both the front and the back cushion pieces, with raw edges aligned and right sides together (fig 6).

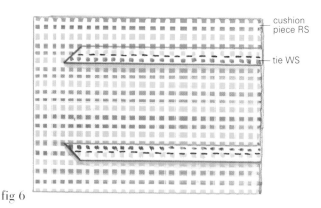

cushion piece RS

tie WS

fig 6

b Place the facings right side down over the ties along the opening edge, with raw edges aligned. Using a 1.5 cm (⅝ in) seam allowance, stitch along this edge (fig 7).

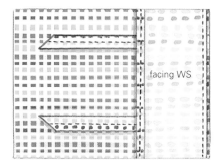

facing WS

fig 7

c Turn the facings to the wrong side and press (fig 8).

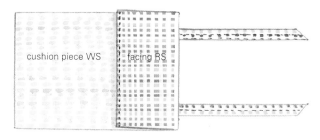

cushion piece WS   facing RS

fig 8

5 If the cushion is to be closed with buttons, attach the facings as in steps 4b and 4c above. Stitching through both the cushion piece and the facing, make two or three buttonholes along the front cushion piece opening. With the right side of the facing uppermost, attach corresponding buttons to the back cushion piece (fig 9).

fig 9

6 With right sides together and raw edges aligned, stitch the remaining three sides of the cushion. Snip the corners, turn right side out and press. Insert the inner pad.

FOR THIS SPECIAL EFFECT, CUT OUT THE FRONT AND
BACK CUSHION PIECES. CUT FOUR TRIANGLES TO FIT
THE CUSHION FRONT, ADDING 2 CM (⅜ IN) ALL
ROUND. HEM TWO SIDES OF EACH TRIANGLE. PIN
ALL FOUR TRIANGLES TO THE BACK PIECE WITH
RIGHT SIDES TOGETHER AND RAW EDGES ALIGNED.
PLACE THE FRONT PIECE OVER THE BACK PIECE
WITH RIGHT SIDES TOGETHER. STITCH LEAVING A
SMALL OPENING. TURN RIGHT SIDE OUT, PRESS
CAREFULLY, INSERT THE INNER AND SLIPSTITCH THE
OPENING CLOSED. BRING THE FOUR TRIANGLES
TOGETHER TO MEET IN THE CENTRE OF THE FRONT
PIECE AND STITCH IN PLACE. STITCH A COVERED
BUTTON OVER THE JOIN TO COMPLETE THE COVER.

▲

frilled cushion

Frills may be simple or, with the addition of lace, binding or ribbon, very ornate. The fullness of a frill is usually two and a half times that of the circumference of the cushion. Follow the formula on page 14 to calculate the amount of fabric required. Any trims should be attached to the frill before it is attached to the cushion.

ABOVE   A simple frill is suitable for busy-patterned fabrics.

ABOVE   Frills can be pleated for a more formal effect.

1 To make the cushion cover, cut two pieces of fabric to the required size, adding a 1.5 cm (⅝ in) seam allowance all round.

2 For a centre-back zip, cut the back pieces and attach the zip as instructed on page 91.

3 If piping is required, attach to the right side of the front piece (see page 12).

4 Establish the width and length of the frill (see page 14) and cut the strips accordingly. Join these strips to form one circular piece (fig 10). Stitch and gather the frill as instructed on page 14.

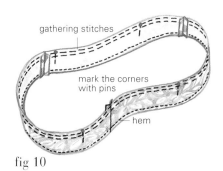

gathering stitches

mark the corners with pins

hem

fig 10

94

ABOVE A folded frill is suitable for reversible cushions. Here the strips are cut twice the required finished width plus a 3 cm (1¼ in) seam allowance. The strips are folded lengthwise and the gathered raw edges are enclosed when the cushion pieces are sewn together.

5 With right sides together and raw edges aligned, pin the frill to the front piece (fig 11). Spread the gathers evenly and tack into position.

6 Place the back cushion piece over the front piece, with right sides together, raw edges aligned and zip opened (fig 12). Pin and stitch.

7 Trim the seams, remove the gathering stitches and turn to the right side. Press, and insert the inner pad.

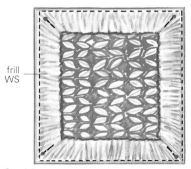

frill
WS

fig 11

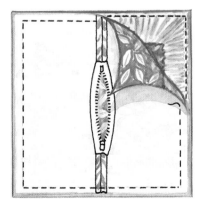

fig 12

oxford-flap cushion

A single flat border (Oxford-flap) is attractive in its simplicity and adds a tailored appearance to the cushion. The width of the flap is usually 5–7 cm (2–2¾ in).

1 Measure the inner pad. For the front of the cushion, add your chosen border width to this measurement plus a 1.5 cm (⅝ in) seam allowance all round (fig 13).

2 Before you cut the cushion back, first decide on the type of opening required.

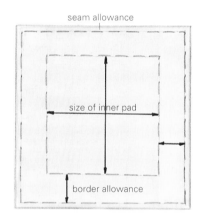

seam allowance

size of inner pad

border allowance

fig 13

a For a zip opening, cut the back in two pieces, adding the border width to the three outside edges and a 1.5 cm (⅝ in) seam allowance all round (fig 14). Insert the zip as instructed on page 10 and open it.

b For an overlapped opening, cut the back in two pieces, adding the border width to the three outside edges, 10 cm (4 in) to the centre-back seams, and a 1.5 cm (⅝ in) seam allowance all round (fig 15).

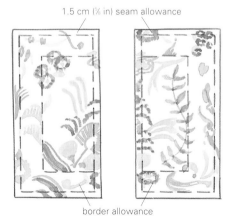

1.5 cm (⅝ in) seam allowance

border allowance

fig 14

overlap   overlap

fig 15

96

With right sides facing raw edges aligned and using a
1.5 cm (⅝ in) seam allowance, pin and stitch the front and
back pieces together. Trim the corners and turn right side out.
Press well, maintaining a neat edge.

Using tailor's chalk, mark the flat border stitching line the
required distance in from the edge (fig 17). Stitch along
the marked line. This stitching may be decorative – for example,
use satin stitch or a double row of stitching, or attach ribbon or
braid to accentuate this line. Insert the inner pad.

If using the overlapped opening, stitch a double-turned
3 cm (1¼ in) hem along both centre-backs. Then overlap
the two back pieces so that the final width of the back equals
that of the front piece (fig 16). Pin in position.

fig 16

fig 17

BOLSTERS

traditionally, bolsters were supporting cushions used as under-pillows on beds and as firm armrests on couches or divans. These days bolsters are used as decorative cushions as well. They can be firm, with a solid foam inner, or yielding and supple, using a soft-filled inner pad. The ends of the bolster may be flat, gathered or tied, depending on the desired effect.

piped bolster with flat ends

1 Establish the circumference and length of the bolster (fig 18). Add a 1.5 cm (⅝ in) seam allowance all round. Cut out the rectangular fabric piece.

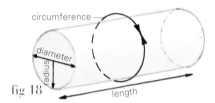

fig 18

2 Measure the diameter of the bolster and add 3 cm (1¼ in) for a seam allowance. Draw a circle of this diameter on paper, then, using this pattern, cut two end pieces of fabric.

3 Staystitch 1.5 cm (⅝ in) in along the side seam lines of the main fabric piece. Snip the seam allowance (fig 19).

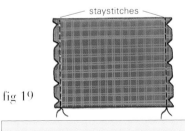

fig 19

STAYSTITCHING THE SEAM LINES PREVENTS YOU FROM CUTTING BEYOND THE STITCH LINE AND ACTS AS A MARKER WHEN YOU ATTACH THE END PIECES.

▲

4 Fold this piece of fabric in half lengthwise, with right sides together and raw edges aligned. Pin and tack (fig 20).

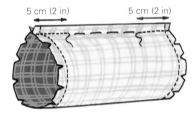

fig 20

5 Machine stitch the top and bottom 5 cm (2 in) of the tacked centre seam, as illustrated above. Press the seam open.

6 Insert the zip – which should be 10 cm (4 in) shorter than the length of the bolster – as instructed on page 10 (fig 21). Remove the tacking and open the zip, keeping the tube wrong side out.

fig 21

7 Attach the piping to the right side of the circular end pieces, snipping the curves (fig 22).

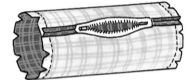

fig 22

8 With right sides together, raw edges aligned and using the staystitching as a guide, pin and stitch the end pieces to the ends of the tube (fig 23). Trim the seams, turn right side out and press. Insert the bolster inner.

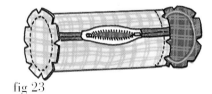

fig 23

98

bolster with gathered ends

This bolster is made from a single, rectangular piece of fabric and the point where the fabric is gathered at each end is disguised with a button or a tassle.

1 To establish the required fabric width, measure the circumference of the bolster inner and add a 3 cm (1¼ in) seam allowance.

2 To establish the required fabric length, measure the length and diameter of the bolster inner, add these together and then add a 6 cm (2¼ in) seam allowance.

3 Cut the fabric accordingly.

4 With right sides together and raw edges aligned, fold the fabric in half lengthwise and stitch. Press the seam open.

5 Should a zip be required, insert as instructed on page 10.

6 Double-turn a 1.5 cm (⅝ in) hem at each end. Stitch, leaving a small opening (fig 24). Turn right side out.

fig 24

7 Insert the bolster inner. Thread string or elastic through the hem at each end, gathering the fabric up as tightly as possible (fig 25). Secure the string or elastic firmly.

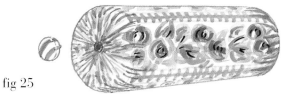

fig 25

8 Conceal this centre point by attaching a tassle or covered button (see page 15).

ABOVE To make a knotted bolster simply construct as for the gathered bolster, but add an extra 50 cm (20 in) to the length for the knot. Gather one end of the bolster, insert the inner and then tie the other end in an attractive knot.

99

CHAIR CUSHIONS

an easy and fairly economical way of transforming a plain kitchen or dining room chair is to dress the seat with an attractive cushion which adds comfort and may be tied onto the chair with decorative ties. Benches and deeper chairs can be enhanced by the addition of comfortable and stylish cushions. The inner pads may be soft and informal or made from shaped foam for a tailored, formal effect. Remember to bear the chair itself in mind before you decide upon a soft or a firm filling, as the style and comfort of the seat should influence your decision: a wrought-iron or wickerwork chair, for example, will need more padding than a comfortable dining room chair.

squab cushion

A squab cushion is designed to fit onto an upright chair. These cushions are fastened to the chair with simple ties or elaborate bows, depending on the effect you wish to create. They are made in the same way as the scatter cushion with a zip opening (page 91), except that the zip is in the side seam and the shape is taken from the seat it is to cover.

1 Make a template of the seat by marking its outline on a large piece of newspaper or tracing paper. Cut around the marked line, and then replace the template on the seat to check the fit.

2 On the template, mark the position of the two back chair struts or legs to establish the best position for the ties.

3 Using the template and adding a 1.5 cm (⅝ in) seam allowance all round, cut two pieces of fabric to form the front and back of the cushion.

4 If a frill is required, prepare as instructed on page 14 and, with right sides together and raw edges aligned, attach it to the front cushion piece.

5 Pin the ties in position on the back edges of the front and back cushion pieces, with raw edges aligned and right sides together. Insert the zip into the seam between the two ties (see page 10), then open the zip.

6 With right sides together and raw edges aligned, stitch the remaining three sides of the cushion. Snip the corners, turn right side out, press and then insert the inner pad.

box cushion

A box cushion is made with a gusset, which adds depth and tailoring. This design is generally used on hard seats or on cane or wicker chairs and benches where extra comfort is important. A foam inner pad is used for a firm cushion because it retains its shape and always looks neat. The depth and density of the foam depends on the style and purpose of the cushion. A soft inner pad needs substantial filling if the cushion is to be effective. Adding piping to the top and bottom seams emphasizes the boxy shape and makes for a neater finish. Choose the piping carefully to tone or contrast with other colours in the cushion, depending on the effect required. The following instructions can be adapted to apply to box cushions of any shape.

1   Measure the inner pad, establishing its length, width and depth (fig 26).

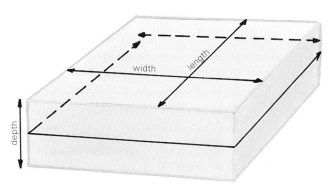

fig 26

2   Make a template the length and width of the pad plus a 1.5 cm (⅝ in) seam allowance all round. Cut two pieces of fabric to fit the template.

3   The gusset is made up of two pieces: the front and sides forming the first piece, and the back, into which the zip is inserted, forming the second. This back piece may be extended around the back corners to allow the inner pad to be removed more easily.

4   The finished width of the gusset is equal to the depth of the inner pad. For the front gusset (including sides) measure the required finished length and width and add a 1.5 cm (⅝ in) seam allowance all round. Cut out.

5   For the back gusset, add 6 cm (2¼ in) to the required finished width, then measure the required finished length and add 3 cm (1¼ in). Cut out.

6   Cut the back gusset in half lengthwise. With right sides together, pin and tack down the length (fig 27).

3 cm (1¼ in)   3 cm (1¼ in)

fig 27

7   Stitch 3 cm (1¼ in) in at each end of this seam as shown above. Press the seam open.

8   Attach the zip as instructed on page 10 (fig 28). The zip should be 6 cm (2¼ in) shorter than the length of the back gusset piece. (Note that if you have lengthened the back gusset piece, the zip will extend around the back corners of the cushion.)

fig 28

9   With right sides together, pin the front and back gusset pieces together at the short ends. Check that the gusset fits around the inner pad and adjust if necessary. Stitch the seams (fig 29).

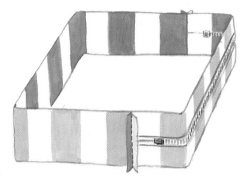

fig 29

10 If piping is required, attach to the right side of the front and back cushion pieces (see page 12), joining the piping at the back of the cushion. Snip the corners of the piping to allow easing.

11 With right sides together, raw edges and corners aligned and the back of the gusset centred, pin and tack the gusset to the back cushion piece.

12 Stitch carefully, turning sharply at the corners and snipping the seams for ease (fig 30).

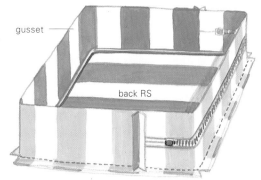

fig 30

13 With the zip open, attach the front piece as instructed in steps 11 and 12 (fig 31).

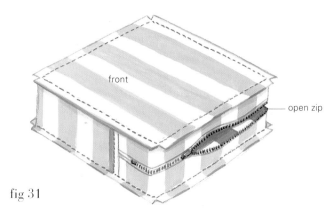

fig 31

14 Turn right side out and press. Insert the inner pad.

quick-and-easy box cushion

This is a simple and much quicker method of making a shaped cushion with a thick inner pad but without a gusset.

1   As illustrated, measure the width and length of the inner pad from the centre of the depth on the one side to the centre of the depth on the other side (fig 32). Add a 1.5 cm (⅝ in) seam allowance all round. Cut two pieces of fabric to this size.

fig 32

2   If piping is required, attach to the right side of the front piece.

3   With right sides together and raw edges aligned, tack together the front and back pieces along the zip seam. Stitch 3 cm (1¼ in) in at each end of this seam. Insert the zip (which should be 6 cm [2¼ in] shorter than the length of the seam) as instructed on page 10.

4   Open the zip. With right sides together and raw edges aligned, pin and tack the three remaining side seams. Stitch and trim the seams (fig 33).

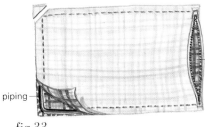

open zip

piping

fig 33

5   Keeping the cover inside out, insert the inner pad.

6   Ensure that the seam is centrally positioned all round and that the zip is nearly closed. Take up the excess fabric at the corners and secure with pins (fig 34).

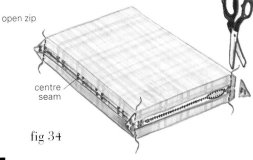

centre seam

fig 34

7   Open the zip, remove the inner pad and stitch each corner along the pinned line as illustrated above.

8   Trim any excess fabric and turn the cover right side out. Press and insert the inner pad.

chair covers

even the simplest, MOST BASIC CHAIR CAN BE EASILY TRANSFORMED INTO AN ATTRACTIVE FEATURE WITH THE ADDITION OF A LOOSE COVER. LOOSE COVERS ARE NOT ONLY AN ECONOMICAL WAY OF CHANGING A ROOM'S DÉCOR, BUT ARE ALSO A PERFECT DISGUISE FOR WORN OR DAMAGED CHAIRS AND SOFAS. THEY MAY ALSO BE USED TO PROTECT EXPENSIVE FABRICS FROM DAILY WEAR AND TEAR. MAKING A COVER IS NOT AS DAUNTING AS YOU MAY THINK, BUT IT IS IMPORTANT FIRST TO MAKE A PATTERN FROM CALICO OR ANOTHER INEXPENSIVE FABRIC. THIS REQUIRES ONLY A BIT MORE TIME AND WORK, BUT ONCE THE PATTERN HAS BEEN MASTERED, MAKING THE CHAIR COVER FROM YOUR CHOSEN FABRIC IS VERY REWARDING.

CHOOSE THE FINAL FABRIC CAREFULLY: THE CORRECT FABRIC WILL PRODUCE A WELL-TAILORED, PROFESSIONAL-LOOKING COVER. IT SHOULD BE WASHABLE, PRE-SHRUNK AND SUFFICIENTLY HARD-WEARING. AVOID LOOSE WEAVES WHICH QUICKLY LOSE THEIR SHAPE. A LARGE-PATTERNED FABRIC MAY LOOK IMPRESSIVE BUT THE MOTIFS MUST BE SYMMETRICAL AND CENTERED, WHICH USES MUCH MORE FABRIC.

RIGHT   Covered buttons finish off this cover with perfect simplicity.

CLASSIC LOOSE COVERS
FOR ARMCHAIRS OR SOFAS

ESTIMATING FABRIC QUANTITIES

Loose covers are cut and pinned together on the chair to ensure a good fit. Errors can be avoided and fabric requirements estimated more accurately by first making a pattern in old sheeting or calico. If you wish to cover the seat cushions separately, remove them before measuring. Five main measurements are required for estimating fabric quantities (fig 1):

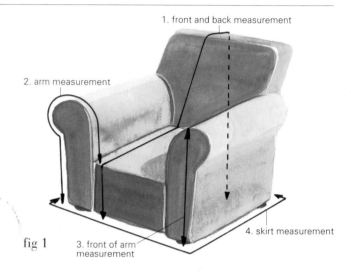

1. front and back measurement

2. arm measurement

fig 1

3. front of arm measurement

4. skirt measurement

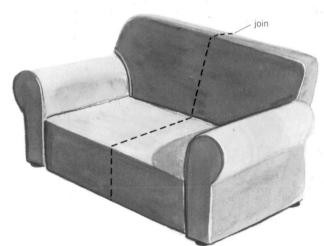

join

fig 2.1

1 **The front and back:** measure from the floor up the back of the chair, over the top, down the front, across the seat and down the front apron to the floor. Include 5 cm (2 in) for each seam crossed and an extra 25 cm (9¾ in) for tuck-ins, as illustrated (fig 1). For a two-seat sofa, multiply this measurement by two or more, depending on the width of the fabric. The panels can either be attached side-by-side (fig 2.1) or on each side of the central panel (fig 2.2).

2 **The arm:** measure from the floor up the outside arm, over the top and down the inner arm. Add 15 cm (6 in) for the tuck-in. Double this figure to allow for both sides.

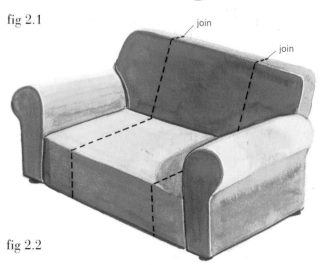

join

join

fig 2.2

3 **The front of the arm:** measure from the floor upwards. The two sides can be cut from one width of fabric.

4 **The skirt:** if the cover needs a skirt, extra fabric is required. First measure the distance all round the chair/sofa. Then decide on the style of skirt and multiply this measurement to accommodate the required fullness: for a gathered skirt (fig 3.1) multiply by two, for a box-pleated skirt (fig 3.2) multiply by three, and for box-pleated corners (fig 3.3) add an extra 40 cm (16 in) for each corner. Decide on the depth of the skirt – this is usually about 15 cm (6 in) – and add 10 cm (4 in) for the seam and hem allowances.

fig 3.1

fig 3.2

fig 3.3

5 **Fitted cushions:** measure right around the cushion (fig 4), adding 5 cm (2 in) for every seam crossed. Multiply this figure by the number of cushions required.

fig 4

MAKING UP THE COVER

Use this technique to make up and perfect the pattern for your chair or sofa. Refer to the measurements established on pages 106–107, and cut out suitably sized pieces of calico. Once you are satisfied that the cover fits well, carefully unpick the calico pattern along all the seams and use each piece as a template from which to cut your chosen fabric.

1 Pin the first piece of fabric firmly to the back of the chair. (If there is a pattern on the fabric, centre the design.) Cut around the shape of the back leaving a 5 cm (2 in) seam allowance. Allow a 10 cm (4 in) hem allowance in the length. If a skirt is to be attached, only a 4 cm (1⅝ in) seam allowance is necessary.

2 Cut a piece of fabric for the front, allowing 10 cm (4 in) for the tuck-in and the seam allowance. Pin firmly to the chair and then pin the front and back pieces together. If the chair back is shaped, gather, pleat or dart the seams together towards the back of the chair (fig 5).

3 Cut the seat fabric, allowing a 10 cm (4 in) tuck-in along the back and sides of the seat and a 5 cm (2 in) seam allowance across the front. Pin it to the front piece (fig 6).

fig 6

4 Cut and then pin the bottom chair front piece to the seat piece, as illustrated, allowing enough in the length for a 10 cm (4 in) hem or a 4 cm (1⅝ in) seam allowance if a skirt is to be attached.

5 Cut the arm panel. Pin the inside section of the arm panel to the seat fabric, allowing for a 10 cm (4 in) tuck-in. Pin to the chair front fabric, shaping around the arm as illustrated (fig 7). It is useful to pin the fabric to the chair to hold it in place.

6 Pin the outside section of the arm panel to the back piece down the side of the chair. Allow for a 10 cm (4 in) hem or a 4 cm (1⅝ in) seam allowance, depending on whether or not a skirt is required.

7 Cut a template of the front of the arm. Use this to cut out two front arms including the required hem and seam allowance (fig 8). Pin in position, making sure that the fit is snug.

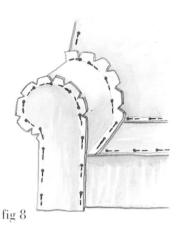

fig 8

8 Remove the pinned cover, carefully turning each seam around and then re-pin with right sides together. Trim the excess fabric leaving a 2 cm (¾ in) seam allowance. Replace the cover on the chair, tucking in the tuck-ins and checking that it fits well, especially over the arms.

9 Remove the cover and stitch all the seams, following the pinning order. Snip the curved seams and press.

10 Place the cover on the chair once again. Measure, mark and pin the hem while the cover is still on the chair.

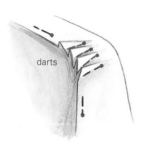

darts

pleats

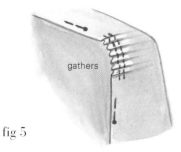

gathers

fig 5

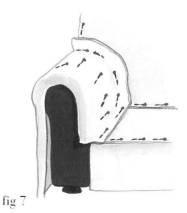

fig 7

11 Should a skirt be required, stitch the hem and then, with the cover in place on the chair, measure the required height of the skirt, marking with either pins or tailor's chalk (fig 9).

fig 9

12 Prepare the skirt, if using, by joining the strips, hemming the lower edge and then either gathering or pleating the top edge as desired (fig 10). Any seams where the skirt has been joined should, if possible, be concealed inside the pleats.

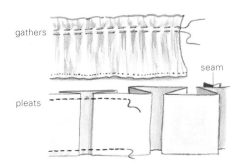

fig 10

13 With right sides together, pin the skirt to the marked line on the cover (fig 11), ensuring, if pleats have been used, that they fall correctly at the corners. Stitch the skirt and press down flat.

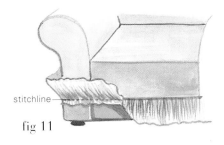

fig 11

ABOVE To neaten the fit of a loose cover, attach ties to the corners.

LOOSE COVERS FOR
HIGH-BACKED CHAIRS

Loose-fitting covers for dining chairs have become very popular. The design of the cover may be either simple, with a centre-back opening to allow for easy removal, or elaborate, with inverted pleats on the corners and coordinating bow ties. For frequently used chairs it is advisable to use washable and fairly hard-wearing fabric. Prewash all fabric to avoid shrinkage of the finished cover. Piping is optional, but will strengthen the seams and neaten the edges.

chair cover with inverted corner pleats

ESTIMATING FABRIC QUANTITIES

1 Take your measurements from the chair you are to cover. Errors can be avoided by first making a pattern in old sheeting or calico; this also allows fabric quantities to be estimated more accurately.

2 With reference to figure 12 alongside, measure the width and length of each panel as follows:

a **Full back panel:** from floor to top of chairback, and across width of back

b **Front panel of back rest:** from top to seat, and across width

c **Seat:** depth and width

d **Side panel x 2:** from seat to floor and across width

e **Front panel:** from seat to floor and across width

3 Add a 3 cm (1¼ in) seam allowance all round to panels A, B and C.

4 On panels D and E, add 45 cm (18 in) to the width for the pleats and 7 cm (2¾ in) to the length for seam and hem allowances.

5 Cut out these six panels, pattern-matching if necessary.

fig 12

111

MAKING UP THE COVER

1 With the wrong sides of the fabric facing outwards, hold the back panel A against the chair. Position the front panel B and pin together (fig 13).

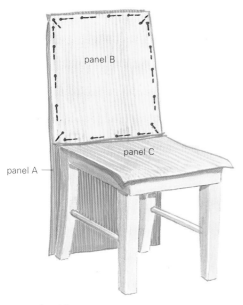

fig 13

2 Square the corners by folding a small dart or pleat.

3 Pin the seat panel C to the front panel B, as illustrated.

4 With right sides together, pin together the vertical seams of the skirt panels D and E (fig 14).

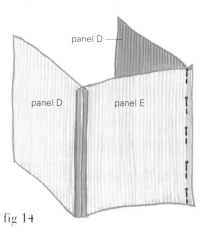

fig 14

5 With right sides together, pin the centre of the front panel E to the centre of the seat panel C. Continue to pin E to C, moving from the centre towards the corners (fig 15).

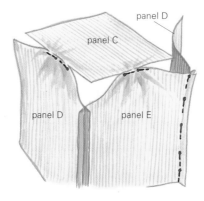

fig 15

6 Fold the excess fabric back to form approximately 10 cm (4 in) pleats at each corner. Pin in position (fig 16).

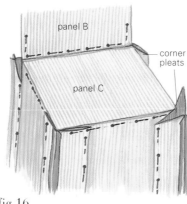

fig 16

7 Pin the side skirt panels D to the back panel A, folding the excess fabric to form approximately 10 cm (4 in) pleats at each corner. Pin in position.

8 Adjust all the seams so that the cover fits comfortably. Mark the seams with tailor's chalk, following the pins accurately.

9 Remove the cover. Separate the pieces, keeping the pleats pinned in position. Trim any excess fabric maintaining a 1.5 cm (⅝ in) seam allowance (fig 17). Do not trim the bottom hemline.

fig 17

10 Attach the piping to the seams where required (see page 12), usually around the chair back and seat (fig 18).

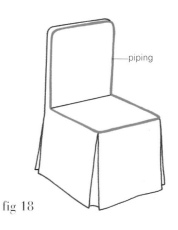

fig 18

11 Stitch the darts and pleats in position.

12 Place right sides together and re-pin the cover along the marked lines. Place it on the chair to make sure that it fits well.

13 Remove from the chair, and stitch the panels together in the following order:

a   Front panel B to seat C;

b   Skirt D and E to seat C, matching the seams to the corners;

c   The back A to the rest of the cover.

14 Trim the seams and turn right side out. Replace the cover on the chair to check the fit.

15 Mark the hemline with pins, making sure the cover hangs straight and is properly positioned.

16 Remove the cover and allow approximately 6 cm (2¼ in) for a 3 cm (1¼ in) double-turned hem. Trim the excess fabric, then stitch and press.

113

ABOVE   Covered buttons have been used to set off and neaten the inverted pleats at the back corners of this loose cover.

ABOVE   Small bowties are positioned to enhance the shape of the Lloyd Loom chair and to add some definition to the loose cover.

ABOVE   Ties of the required length and width may be sewn into the back side seams.

bed linen

the bedroom IS A PERSONAL RETREAT
WHERE INDIVIDUAL PREFERENCE CAN BE INDULGED
IN WITHOUT RESTRAINT. BEFORE CHOOSING A STYLE
AND COLOUR SCHEME, IT IS NECESSARY TO CONSIDER WHETHER TO USE A DUVET
OR SHEETS, BLANKETS AND BEDSPREAD. ONCE THIS HAS BEEN ESTABLISHED, FIBRE
AND TEXTURE CAN BE DECIDED UPON. A WIDE RANGE OF FABRICS IS AVAILABLE,
FROM FEMININE BRODERIE ANGLAISE TO EXOTIC SATIN. MOST PEOPLE SETTLE FOR
COTTON, BRUSHED COTTON OR POLYESTER/COTTON BLENDS, WHICH ARE
REASONABLY INEXPENSIVE AND AVAILABLE IN MANY COLOURS. BY CREATIVE
COORDINATION, COLOURS AND PRINTS CAN BE COMBINED TO FORM A MIX-AND-
MATCH EFFECT. RIBBON, LACE, EMBROIDERY,
PIPING AND OTHER INTERESTING TRIMMINGS
CAN BE USED TO ENHANCE PLAIN FABRIC. A
MOTIF CAN BE COPIED FROM THE CURTAIN, FOR
EXAMPLE, AND APPLIQUÉD ONTO THE DUVET
COVER, PILLOWCASES AND BEDSPREAD FOR A
SPECIAL EFFECT. OR ADD LUXURIOUS DRAPES TO
A CANOPY OR CORONA TO TURN AN ORDINARY
BED INTO A DREAMLAND.

OPPOSITE Clouds of soft muslin draped around the wrought-iron
frame are combined with bright cotton fabrics to give this four-
poster bed a cool, contemporary look.

PILLOWCASES

When making coordinating pillowcases, choose fabric that complements the main pattern of the duvet cover or sheets, one that washes well and that is pleasant to sleep on. Extra-wide sheeting is commercially available and is more economical to use. The style of trimming should also tie in with the overall design of the room.

---

one-piece pillowcase

This plain pillowcase is the simplest type to make, and has a flap inside the opening to hold the pillow in place. Standard pillowcase sizes vary from 45 cm x 70 cm (18 in x 28 in) to 48 cm x 76 cm (19 in x 30 in), so take accurate measurements.

1 Measure the required finished length of the pillow, double this measurement and add 27 cm (10¾ in) for a flap and hem allowance.

2 Measure the required finished width and add a 3 cm (1¼ in) seam allowance.

3 Cut the fabric accordingly.

4 Along one short edge of the fabric, double-turn a 1 cm (⅜ in) hem to the wrong side, press and stitch (fig 1).

5 Along the other short edge, fold first 1 cm (⅜ in) and then another 4 cm (1⅝ in) to the wrong side, press and stitch. (Decorative stitching may be used to add detail to the front of the finished pillowcase.)

6 Lay the fabric flat with the right side up. Fold the narrow hemmed edge over to the right side to form a 20 cm (8 in) flap. Press.

7 Fold the wide hemmed edge over to the right side, placing this edge under the flap to meet at the pressed crease (fig 2). Pin in position.

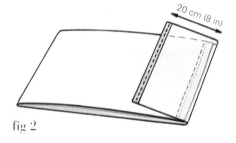

fig 2

8 Stitch the side seams using a 1.5 cm (⅝ in) seam allowance (fig 3). Trim the excess fabric and overlock or zigzag the edges.

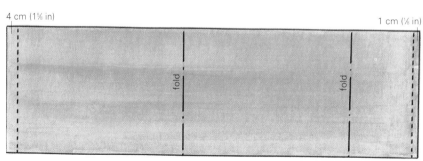

4 cm (1⅝ in)

1 cm (⅜ in)

fold

fold

fig 1

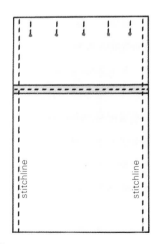

stitchline

stitchline

fig 3

9 Turn the pillowcase to the right side and press.

118

THREE-PIECE PILLOWCASE

IF THE FABRIC IS NOT WIDE ENOUGH TO CUT THE PILLOWCASE IN ONE PIECE, SEPARATE THE PIECES ON THE FOLD LINES, ALLOWING AN EXTRA 1.5 CM (⅝ IN) SEAM ALLOWANCE WHERE THE PIECES WILL BE JOINED. STITCH TOGETHER AND PROCEED WITH STEP 4.

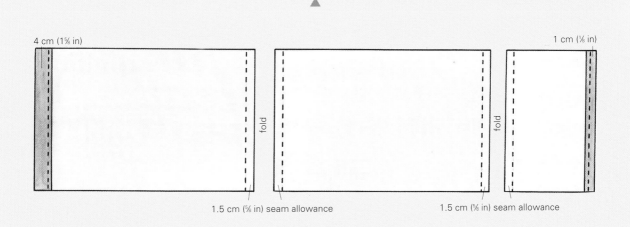

4 cm (1⅝ in)

1 cm (⅛ in)

fold

fold

1.5 cm (⅝ in) seam allowance

1.5 cm (⅝ in) seam allowance

FRILLED PILLOWCASE

ADD FRILLS FOR A FEMININE TOUCH OR SOFT COUNTRY EFFECT. LACE, BORDERS OR CONTRASTING FRILLS MAY BE USED, OR EVEN DOUBLE FRILLS OF VARIOUS WIDTHS – THE OPTIONS ARE ENDLESS. SEE SEWING TECHNIQUES, PAGE 14, FOR FRILL INSTRUCTIONS.

oxford-flap pillowcase

This popular style of pillowcase with its flat border provides a simple, elegant finish to bed linen. Beds which display these pillowcases need no further adornment. They are not complicated to make but need to be cut accurately. These instructions allow for a 5 cm (2 in) Oxford border.

1 Measure the required finished length of the pillow, double this measurement, add 27 cm (10¾ in) for the flap and hem allowance, plus an extra 20 cm (8 in) for the Oxford borders.

2 Measure the required finished width of the pillow and add a 3 cm (1¼ in) seam allowance plus 10 cm (4 in) for the Oxford borders (fig 4).

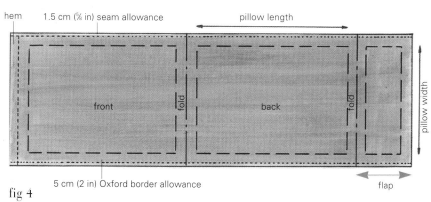

fig 4

3 Cut fabric accordingly. If the fabric is not wide enough to cut the pillowcase in one piece, follow the instructions in the box on page 119.

4 Along one short edge of the fabric, double-turn a 1 cm (⅜ in) hem to the wrong side, press and stitch.

5 Along the other short edge, fold first 1 cm (⅜ in) and then another 4 cm (1⅝ in) to the wrong side, press and stitch.

6 Lay the fabric flat with the right side up. Fold the narrow hemmed edge over to the right side to form a flap of 25 cm (9¾ in). (This includes the 5 cm [2 in] Oxford flap border.) Press.

7 Fold the wide hemmed edge over to the right side, placing this edge under the flap and making sure that the edge lies 6 cm (2¼ in) away from the pressed crease of the flap (fig 5). (This is so that the pillowcase opening is not caught when the border is stitched.) Pin in position.

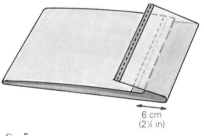

6 cm
(2¼ in)

fig 5

8 Stitch the side seams using a 1.5 cm (⅝ in) seam allowance (fig 6). Trim the excess fabric and overlock or zigzag the edges.

1.5 cm (⅝ in) seam allowance

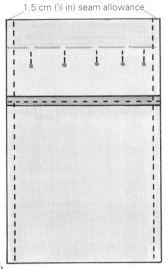

fig 6

9 Turn the pillowcase to the right side and press the seams carefully.

TO EMPHASIZE THE FLAT BORDER USE A DECORATIVE STITCH, SUCH AS SATIN STITCH, OR ADD A TRIM, SUCH AS RIBBON OR LACE.

▲

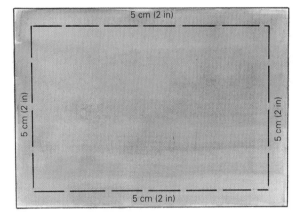

5 cm (2 in)

5 cm (2 in)

5 cm (2 in)

5 cm (2 in)

fig 7

10 Using tailor's chalk, mark the border exactly 5 cm (2 in) in from the edge on all four sides (fig 7).

Stitch carefully along this marked line, making sure that the back opening is not sewn closed (fig 8).

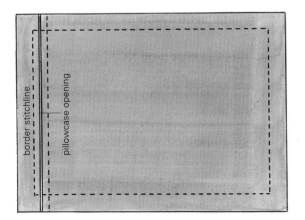

border stitchline

pillowcase opening

fig 8

continental pillowcase

Continental pillows are extra-large, square cushions used on a bed for added comfort or purely as a design feature. If they are to be functional, simple piped pillowcases are recommended. However, if they are intended to be only decorative, any amount of detail may be added. The standard sizes of continental pillowcases vary from 65 cm x 65 cm (26 in x 26 in) to 80 cm x 80 cm (31 in x 31 in). To make up, measure your pillow carefully before you begin, and then follow the instructions given for the one-piece pillowcase (page 118).

FITTED SHEETS

$f$itted sheets are neater and more economical than flat sheets. Sheeting, most suitable because of its extra width and because it is easy to launder, is available in cotton as well as in polyester/cotton blends. Other fabrics may be used, such as brushed cotton or flannelette, which are cosy to sleep on, or cotton Percale, a fine cotton weave, which is expensive but of very high quality. Use satin for an exotic touch! Choose the colour of the fabric to coordinate with the rest of your bed linen.

1 To calculate the amount of fabric required, measure the length and width of the mattress (fig 9). Add the depth of the mattress x 2 plus a 36 cm (14⅛ in) tuck-in allowance to each of these two measurements (this allows for a tuck-in of 18 cm [7 in] all round).

2 Cut the fabric as calculated. From each corner, measure out the depth of the mattress plus the 18 cm (7 in) tuck-in and mark (see fig 10). Measure this same distance at right angles to these marks and then join the lines to form a square. Mark a 1 cm (⅜ in) seam allowance along the inside of each square and cut out.

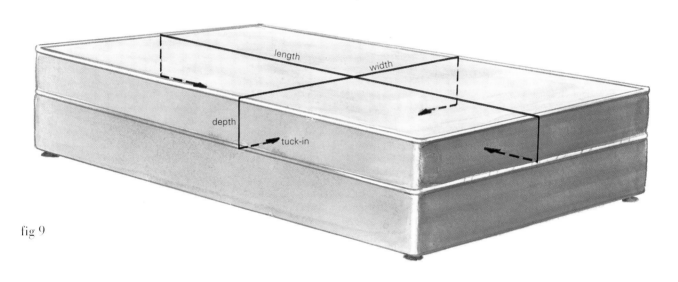

fig 9

E X A M P L E

SINGLE BED

Length of mattress = 188 cm (74 in)
Depth of mattress = 17 cm (6¾ in) x 2 = 34 cm (13½ in)
Tuck-in   = 36 cm (14⅛ in)
Cutting Length = 258 cm (101⅝ in)
Width of mattress = 91 cm (36⅜ in)
Depth of mattress = 17 cm (6¾ in) x 2 = 34 cm (13½ in)
Tuck-in   = 36 cm (14⅛ in)
Cutting Width = 161 cm (64 in)

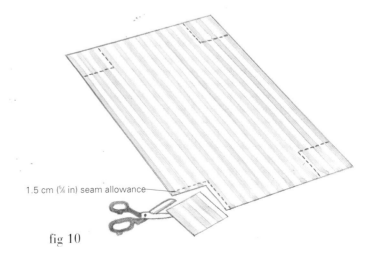

1.5 cm (⅝ in) seam allowance

fig 10

3 With right sides facing, pin these cut edges together. Using a 1 cm (⅜ in) seam allowance, stitch the seams and then overlock or zigzag the raw edges (fig 11).

6 To gather the corners, thread narrow elastic in through one of the gaps at each corner and stitch firmly in place. Thread the elastic out through the adjacent gap and pull it taut to gather the corner, and then stitch securely (fig 13). Stitch the gaps in the hem closed.

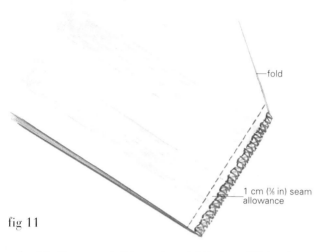

fold

1 cm (⅜ in) seam allowance

fig 11

4 Working around all four edges, fold in 1 cm (⅜ in) and then another 2 cm (¾ in) to the wrong side to form a hem. Press and pin in position.

5 Measure 15 cm (6 in) along the hem on each side of all four corners and mark. Stitch along the hem leaving an open gap at these marks (fig 12).

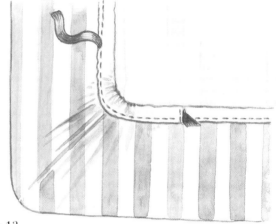

fig 13

FOR AN ATTRACTIVE MATTRESS COVER ON A DAYBED, MAKE A FITTED SHEET IN A THICKER FABRIC THAN USUAL AND ONE WHICH HAS AN INTERESTING DESIGN.

▲

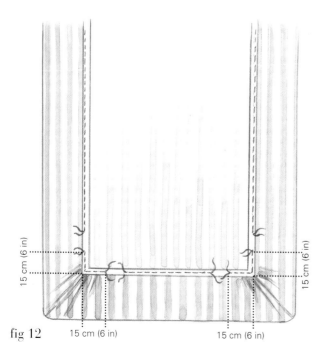

15 cm (6 in)

15 cm (6 in)

fig 12   15 cm (6 in)   15 cm (6 in)

DUVET COVERS

duvets, or continental quilts as they are otherwise known, are not only convenient to use, making top sheets, blankets and bedcovers unnecessary, but are also warm and light. A variety of fillings can be used, such as down, feathers or a combination of the two, or even synthetic fillings for allergy sufferers. The covers too can be made from a variety of fabrics. If the desired fabric is not suitable for sleeping against, substitute the back piece of the duvet cover with a matching sheeting fabric. The style of the duvet cover can be adapted to suit the bedroom décor. As duvet sizes vary considerably, and the fullness of the duvet itself may also vary depending on the filling used, measure your duvet carefully before you begin.

simple duvet cover

This type of duvet cover is constructed like a very large pillowcase. The opening may be closed in a number of ways, varying from practical Velcro strips or press studs to decorative ties or buttons.

1   To calculate fabric quantities, measure the required length of the cover, double this measurement, and add 37 cm (14⅝ in) for the flap and hem allowances.

2   Measure the required finished width and add a 3 cm (1¼ in) seam allowance.

3   Cut the fabric accordingly. If the duvet is wider than the fabric, join pieces to each side of the centre panel, pattern-matching if necessary (see page 31).

4   Along one short edge of the fabric, double-turn a 1 cm (⅜ in) hem to the wrong side, press and stitch.

5   Along the other short edge, fold first 1 cm (⅜ in) and then another 4 cm (1⅝ in) to the wrong side, press and stitch.

oxford-flap duvet cover

Make this style of duvet cover exactly as instructed for the Oxford-flap pillowcase on page 120. To calculate the quantities of fabric required, merely adapt the sizes and complete as instructed for the pillowcase. The size of the Oxford-flap border may be increased to as much as 8–10 cm (3¼–3½ in).

BEDCOVERS

the most popular bedcover is the easy, throwover bedspread. Throwovers can vary from a simple, single piece of hemmed fabric to an elaborate quilt with a rolled edge. They may cover the bed completely, touching the floor all round or, if a bed valance (nightfrill) is to be exposed, the throwover can hang to just below the mattress.

throwover with a rolled edge

This throwover may be lined or unlined – the method remains the same for both, as the lining and fabric together are treated as one piece. Decide before you begin to make the throwover whether you wish it to hang to the floor or just below the mattress. The size of the roll may vary.

1   To calculate the amount of fabric required, measure the length and width of the made-up bed. Add the required length of overhang x 2, plus 5 cm (2 in) for the rolled edge and a 3 cm (1¼ in) seam allowance to both the length and the width. If a tuck under the pillow is required, add an extra 50 cm (20 in) to the length (fig 16).

2   Cut out the fabric and lining, if using, to fit these dimensions. If the throwover is wider than the fabric, join panels on each side of the centre panel, pattern-matching if necessary (see page 31). Round off the corners.

3   Measure down one long side of the fabric, across the width at the bottom and back up the other long side to calculate the required length of the rolled edge. Cut sufficient 15 cm (6 in) wide strips of fabric to fit this measurement plus a little extra for the end seams when joined together. Stitch the strips together.

4   Cut a corresponding length of wadding strips – these should be 5 cm (2 in) wide for a medium roll or 10 cm (4 in) wide for a chunkier roll.

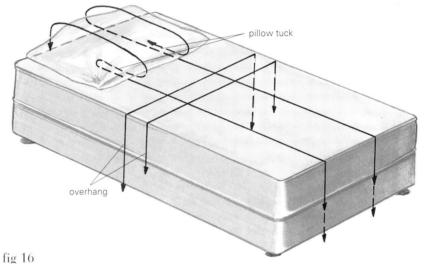

pillow tuck

overhang

fig 16

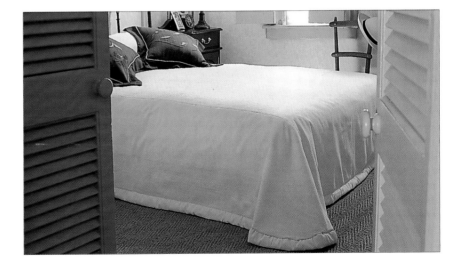

129

5 Place the lining, if using, on top of the throwover fabric with wrong sides facing and raw edges aligned.

6 Along the top edge, double-turn a 2 cm (¾ in) hem and stitch, stitching the fabric and lining, if using, together.

7 Position the wadding on the wrong side of the prepared fabric strip for the rolled edge. Fold the strip in half lengthwise with the right side out to enclose the wadding, and stitch 1 cm (⅜ in) from the edge.

8 With right sides facing and raw edges aligned, pin the roll to the three sides of the throwover measured in step 3, easing it around the corners and allowing the ends of the roll to overlap the edges of the throwover slightly (fig 17). Stitch the roll in place.

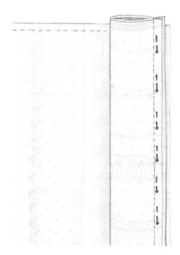

fig 17

9 Trim the excess fabric and overlock or zigzag the raw edges. If the fabric has a tendency to fray easily, bind the raw edges with bias binding.

10 Turn in the raw edges at the ends of the roll and slipstitch closed (fig 18).

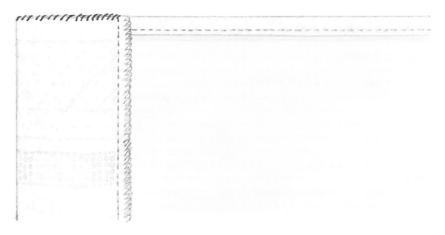

fig 18

ABOVE   A heavy bullion fringe can be added to the throwover instead of a padded roll.

130

BED VALANCES

a bed valance (or nightfrill as it is sometimes known) serves as an attractive cover to conceal the bed base and legs. If you choose fabric which coordinates with your bed linen and curtaining, it can provide the perfect complement to your bedroom decorating scheme. The style of the valance can be varied to great effect: a gently gathered valance softens the line of the bed, while one which is tailored and box-pleated gives a smart appearance, and a quilted, fitted valance can serve to simulate a rich, upholstered bed base. The basic method of construction for all of these valances is the same: lining bordered with fabric to match the valance is used as the base cover under the mattress, and the valance is varied according to your requirements. Accurate measurements are essential for a successful valance.

MAKING UP THE BASE COVER AND BORDER

1 Measure the width and length of the bed base (fig 19).

2 Add a 3 cm (1¼ in) seam allowance to both the length and the width of the bed base and cut out in lining fabric.

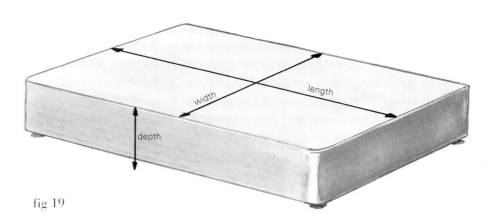

fig 19

3 For the border, use fabric to match the valance fabric. Cut two 15 cm (6 in) wide fabric strips for the sides to equal the length of the lining. Cut a 15 cm (6 in) wide fabric strip for the bottom to equal the width of the lining.

4 Join these three strips (ensuring that the side strips are attached on either side of the bottom strip [fig 20]), making mitred corners as instructed on pages 12–13.

mitred corners

fig 20

5 Lay this border over the lining fabric to check that it fits exactly. Fold in 1 cm (⅜ in) to the wrong side along the inside of the border (as illustrated in fig 20). Press and then set aside.

6 Double-turn a 1 cm (⅜ in) hem along the top edge of the lining, press and stitch.

ABOVE A quilted, fitted bed valance simulates the effect of a richly upholstered bed base and, at the same time, hides the mattress and legs.

MAKING UP A GATHERED BED VALANCE

1 For the required finished length of the valance, measure down the length of the bed, across the width, and back up the length. Multiply this by 2 to 2.5 depending on the fullness required. To calculate the number of drops, divide this figure by the width of the fabric and round up to the nearest whole number.

2 To calculate the depth of the valance, measure the height from the floor to the top of the bed base (see figure 19 on page 131) and add 7.5 cm (3 in) for seam and hem allowances.

3 Multiply the number of drops by the depth of the valance (including allowances) to calculate the fabric required for the frill. If required, allow for pattern-matching as instructed on page 31.

4 Cut the required number of drops and join with overlocked or French seams, pattern-matching if necessary (see page 31).

5 Double-turn 2 cm (¾ in) side hems. Press, pin and stitch.

6 Double-turn a 3 cm (1¼ in) bottom hem. Press, pin and stitch.

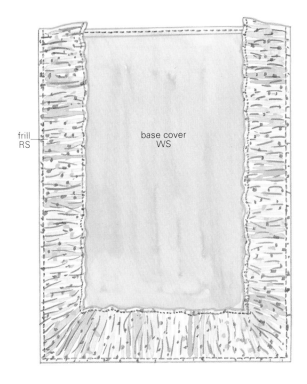

frill
RS

base cover
WS

fig 21

7 Stitch two rows of gathering stitches about 1 cm (⅜ in) from the top edge, as instructed on page 8. Gather up the valance to the required finished length, distributing the gathers evenly.

8 Making sure that the **wrong sides** are facing and the raw edges aligned, pin the valance to the prepared base cover (fig 21). Check that it fits the bed base comfortably. Tack and stitch the valance in position.

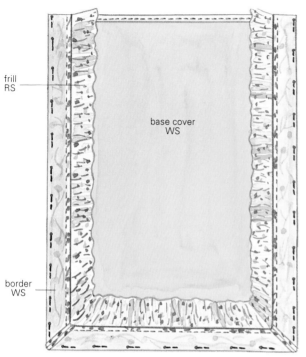

fig 22

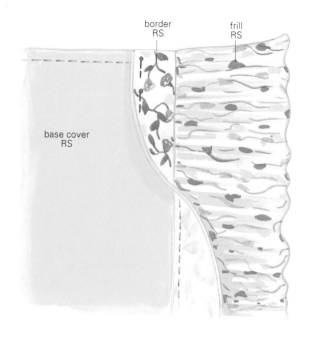

fig 23

9 Place the base cover flat with the wrong side up, and fold the valance in so that it is right side up. Place the prepared border over the valance, so that the right sides are facing and raw edges aligned. Pin, tack and stitch in position (fig 22). Trim any excess fabric and remove gathering stitches.

10 Lay the base cover and valance right side up flat on a large surface. (If possible, place the bed valance on the bed base and work accurately from here.) Fold the border towards the centre of the base cover to enclose the raw edges (fig 23) so that it is flat and right side up. Carefully pin and tack the loose hemmed edge of the border to the base cover, and then stitch neatly (fig 24).

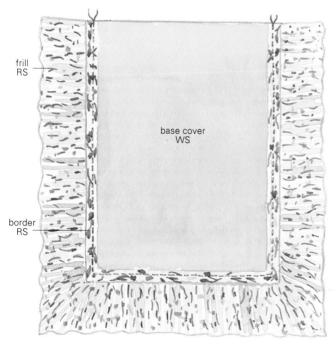

fig 24

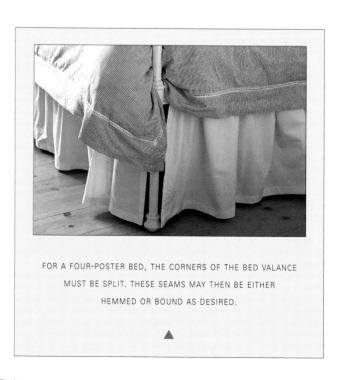

FOR A FOUR-POSTER BED, THE CORNERS OF THE BED VALANCE MUST BE SPLIT. THESE SEAMS MAY THEN BE EITHER HEMMED OR BOUND AS DESIRED.

FOUR-POSTER BEDS

The traditional four-poster bed has a romantic charm of its own, and can be dressed in many ways. A combination of curtains, valance and canopy is most common, but all three are not always used together. Bed curtains which can be tied back to the bedposts may be used alone to add a feeling of warmth and enclosure. Allow the style and era of the bed to influence your choice of dressing: brass beds often have a valance only to expose the beauty of the brass frame; on the other hand, simple wooden frames can be elaborately dressed. The look need not, however, always be nostalgic: the draping of soft muslin around a modern wrought-iron or wooden framework can create a contemporary, cool, ethereal look. Because both sides are visible, the curtains and the valance should be lined with either the same fabric or a coordinating lining. The type of frame and fittings will also influence the method of construction.

ruched curtain valance on a rod

1 The curtain valance is made in four pieces, which will each be threaded onto the corresponding rod. To establish the required finished length of each valance section, measure the distances between the bedposts. Multiply by 2 to 2.5 for the required fullness.

2 To calculate the number of drops required for each valance section, divide the figure established in step 1 by the width of the fabric.

3 Decide on the required finished depth of the valance; it should be in proportion to the length of any mock bed-curtains and the size of the bed.

4 For a lined valance, cut the drops of fabric the required finished depth plus 13 cm (5¼ in) for the casing and seam allowances. Cut the lining the same size. For a self-lined valance, cut the drops double the required finished depth plus 20 cm (8 in) for the casing and seam allowances.

5 Join the drops with open seams (see page 9). Double-turn 2 cm (¾ in) side hems. Press and stitch.

6 For the lined valance, join the lining to the fabric along the bottom edge with right sides together.

7 Fold the valance in half lengthwise with right sides together and raw edges aligned. Stitch along the top seam (fig 25). Turn the valance to the right side and press neatly.

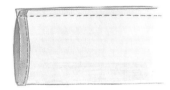

fig 25

8 Measure the width of the rod to establish the required width of the casing. Measuring from the bottom edge

of the valance upwards, first mark the required finished depth of the valance, and then mark the required width of the casing. Stitch along these lines to form the casing (fig 26. The remaining fabric above the casing will form a small frill.

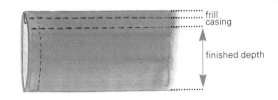

fig 26

9 Thread each valance section through the casing onto its corresponding rod.

IF CURTAINS ARE REQUIRED AND ARE TO SHARE THE SAME ROD AS THE VALANCE, MAKE UP EACH CURTAIN AND ATTACH IT IN STEP 8 TO THE TOP SEAM OF THE CORRESPONDING VALANCE SECTION. STITCH THE CASING THROUGH BOTH THE CURTAIN AND VALANCE.

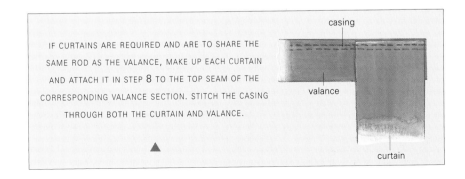

traditional dressing of a four-poster bed

This type of treatment is best suited to wooden framed four-poster beds, which usually have some form of track attached to the inside of the frame from which to hang the curtain, and another track for the valance. Some very formal four-posters require a canopy, usually consisting of fabric attached to the wooden frame and stretched across the top of the bed. A wrought-iron four-poster bed, on the other hand, is better suited to a less formal look: use clouds of soft muslin draped around the frame for a cool yet romantic look (see pages 68–71 for further information about informal swags and draping).

1 For the curtain valance, measure the length of the four sides of the frame, decide on the required heading and proceed to make up the valance by following the instructions on page 59. Hang the valance on the track.

2 For the curtains, measure the length from the track to the floor and proceed to make up the curtains by following the instructions for lined curtains on page 42, 43 or 44. Because the lining will be visible, be sure to choose an appealing fabric. Hang a curtain drop on each corner of the bed.

3 For a flat canopy, cut a rectangular piece of fabric to fit across the top of the frame plus a 2 cm (¾ in) hem allowance all round. Double-turn a 1 cm (⅜ in) hem all round the edges and stitch. Attach to the wooden frame with staples, tacks or hooks, if available.

4 For a gathered canopy, cut a piece of fabric measuring the width of the frame and twice the length plus a 2 cm (¾ in) hem allowance all round. Double-turn and stitch a 1 cm (⅜ in) hem all round the edges. Attach standard (rufflette) curtain heading tape down the length of the canopy on each side. Gather up the tape to fit the wooden frame and attach the canopy to the frame with staples, tacks or hooks, if available.

CORONAS

a corona is a coronet-styled canopy installed above a bed. Simpler to create and dress than a four-poster bed. it can be draped with fabric which flows down behind the bedhead for an extravagant. luxurious effect. Use elaborate trims and rich fabric to add to this ornate impression. On the other hand. use a soft fabric for the simple corona variation.

1 For the corona fitting, cut out a semi-circular piece of wood or chipboard with a diameter of 50–60 cm (20–24 in).

2 Attach a curtain track, screw eyes or standard (rufflette) tape to the curved front edge of the corona from which to hang the two front curtains.

3 Attach screw eyes to the underside of the back from which to hang the back curtain (fig 27).

4 Establish the position of the corona and attach it firmly to the wall using two angle brackets.

5 Measure and make up lined curtains as instructed in chapter 1, page 42, 43 or 44. Ensure that the lining fabric is appealing.

6 Attach tiebacks or holdbacks to the wall with which to hold back the curtains.

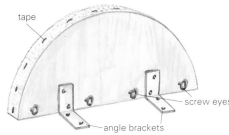

fig 27

ABOVE To make the coronet over the corona. adapt and cover a Tiffany lampshade frame. The drapes of the corona are permanently secured by decorative holdbacks.

SIMPLE CORONA

Using an end socket or angle bracket, attach a short pole (approximately 50 cm [20 in] long) with an attractive finial to the wall above the bed. Drape or ruche a lined and hemmed piece of fabric onto the pole, and secure it with tiebacks or holdbacks.

eight

table linen

decorating your table IS A SIMPLE AND OFTEN INEXPENSIVE WAY TO ENHANCE THE AMBIENCE OF A ROOM, REGARDLESS OF WHETHER THE TABLE IS THE FOCAL POINT OF THE ROOM OR MERELY A SIDE TABLE IN YOUR HALL OR BEDROOM. COORDINATE THE FABRICS YOU CHOOSE TO COMPLEMENT THE DÉCOR OF THE ROOM, AND USE MATS AND NAPKINS AS COLOURFUL ACCENTS. FOR AN ATTRACTIVE DINING TABLE, USE DECORATIVE TABLE LINEN MADE OF A FABRIC WHICH FLATTERS THE TABLEWARE AND BLENDS IN WELL WITH THE OTHER FURNISHINGS. FOR INSTANCE, MODERN CUTLERY AND STURDY CHINA BENEFIT FROM BOLD COLOURS AND EQUALLY MODERN FABRIC DESIGNS. TO PROTECT A TABLECLOTH, ESPECIALLY IN A BEDROOM OR SITTING ROOM, FIT A PIECE OF GLASS CUT TO THE SHAPE OF THE TABLE TOP OVER THE CLOTH. CHOOSE FULLY WASHABLE, PRE-SHRUNK FABRIC WHICH LAUNDERS AND IRONS WELL, AS IT WILL BE SUBJECTED TO MUCH WEAR AND TEAR. EXPERIMENT WITH CREATIVE EMBROIDERY AND OTHER SEWING SKILLS TO ADD A PERSONAL TOUCH.

OPPOSITE   The napkins and table mats combine to complement the rustic charm of the sturdy cutlery and crockery.

TABLECLOTHS

square and rectangular tablecloths

There are no hard and fast rules concerning the correct size of a tablecloth: it should complement the table and be pleasing to the eye. Establish the length of the overhang, which should fall to your lap when you are seated at the table.

3 For an ordinary hem, double-turn 1 cm (⅜ in) to the wrong side all round and stitch.

4 For the wider hem with mitred corners, double-turn a 2.5 cm (1 in) hem to the wrong side all round. Mitre the corners (see pages 12–13). Stitch the hem using either a plain stitch or a decorative satin stitch.

THE CORNERS OF A FLOOR-LENGTH TABLECLOTH WILL DRAPE ON THE FLOOR UNLESS THE CLOTH IS FITTED. PROTECT THE TABLE WITH A HEATPROOF UNDER-CLOTH PLACED BENEATH THE TABLECLOTH.

▲

1 Measure the width and length of the table (fig 1), and add the required overhang measurement to all sides plus a 2 cm (¾ in) hem allowance for an ordinary hem or a 5 cm (2 in) hem allowance for a wider hem with mitred corners. Cut to size.

2 If the tablecloth is wider than the fabric you are using, buy double the quantity you would normally require. Join panels on each side of the centre panel using an open seam and pattern-matching if necessary. Add the required hem allowance all round. Cut to size.

length width

seat-length overhang

floor-length overhang

fig 1

circular tablecloths

A floor-length circular cloth on a side table can brighten up a room, especially when topped by a coordinating, smaller cloth. This smaller cloth may be square or round. Edge either the main cloth or the overcloth with a variety of trims, such as lace, fringing, frills, a padded roll or even piping, depending on the required effect.

A softly padded roll uses thin wadding.

Bullion fringing adds weight to the edges.

A super-imposed frill is very effective.

Bias binding provides a contrasting trim.

fig 2

TO PREVENT THE HEM FROM TWISTING, ADD ONLY A VERY NARROW HEM ALLOWANCE OF 0.5–1 CM (³⁄₁₆–³⁄₈ IN). OVERLOCK THE RAW EDGE, FOLD TO THE WRONG SIDE AND STITCH FLAT.

▲

1   Establish the required length of the overhang, which may fall to your lap when you are seated at the table, or to the floor (fig 2).

2   Measure the diameter of the table, then add twice the overhang and a 4 cm (1⅝ in) hem allowance to this measurement (this is the cutting diameter).

3   Before cutting the fabric into a circle, cut it into a square with sides equalling the cutting diameter measurement established in step 2 above.

4   If the fabric is not wide enough, join panels to each side of the centre panel, using an open seam and pattern-matching if necessary (fig 3). Press flat. Cut the joined fabric to the required square size.

5   Find the centre of the cloth by folding the fabric in half and then in half again.

6   Tie a piece of string measuring half the cutting diameter to tailor's chalk or a pencil. Pin the string at the folded corner (A) and draw an arc (B), keeping the chalk or pencil at right angles to the fabric and keeping the string taut (fig 4). Cut along this arc.

fig 4

7   Double-turn a 1 cm (⅜ in) hem all round the edge. Press and stitch.

TO CALCULATE THE CIRCUMFERENCE OF A ROUND TABLECLOTH IN ORDER TO ESTABLISH HOW MUCH TRIM IS REQUIRED, MULTIPLY THE DIAMETER OF THE CLOTH BY 3.14. FOR EXAMPLE, 180 CM (71 IN) X 3.14 = 565 CM (6 YD 7 IN) TRIM REQUIRED.

▲

IF A FRILL IS REQUIRED, SUBTRACT TWICE THE WIDTH OF THE FRILL FROM THE CUTTING DIAMETER (SEE STEP 2). CALCULATE THE CIRCUMFERENCE OF THE CLOTH USING THE FORMULA IN THE BOX ABOVE, MULTIPLY THIS BY 2.25 FOR FULLNESS, AND PROCEED TO MAKE UP THE FRILL AS INSTRUCTED ON PAGE 14.

▲

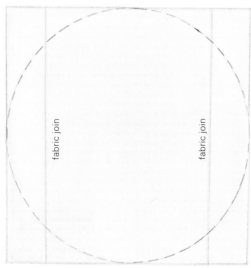

fig 3

ABOVE A fitted tablecloth with inverted pleats is suitable for both square and rectangular tables. Cut the top piece of fabric to fit the tabletop plus a 1.5 cm (⅝ in) seam allowance all round. Cut the skirt separately, allowing an extra 40 cm (16 in) on each corner for the pleats. Place the top piece right side down on the table. With right sides together pin the skirt to the top piece. Fold the extra fabric on the corners back to form approximately 10 cm (4 in) deep pleats, and pin. Stitch the seams, trim any excess fabric, and press. Turn right side out and replace on the table. Mark the hemline with pins, allowing for a 3 cm (1¼ in) double-turned hem. Trim, stitch and then press.

TABLE NAPKINS

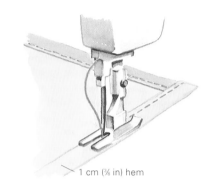

1 cm (⅜ in) hem

fig 5

able napkins can be any size. but they are usually no smaller than 30 cm (12 in) square and no bigger than 45 cm (18 in) square. However. to prevent wastage consider the width of the fabric when deciding upon the size of the napkin. The fabric should also be fully washable and colourfast. A basic napkin has a 1 cm (⅜ in) or smaller double-turned hem (fig 5). Different trims and finishes may be used to create a variety of effects: stitch lace or braid around the hemmed edges: trim the raw edges with bias binding: scallop the corners of the napkin using a small plate as a template. and then satin stitch the raw edges: stitch just inside the edges and then fray the raw edges all round to form a fringe: or appliqué a design onto a corner of each hemmed napkin.

TABLE MATS

add drama and vitality to a table setting by using contrasting colours and patterns, or set off an attractive table with plain and simple table mats. Mats may also be coordinated with the tablecloth to define the place setting. The options are endless. Whatever style you choose, ensure that the fabric and matching trims are fully washable, colourfast and pre-shrunk. The standard size of a rectangular table mat is 20 cm x 30 cm (8 in x 12 in). Round table mats may have a diameter of 25–30 cm (9¾–14 in). However, provided that the table is big enough, larger mats may look very effective.

simple quilted table mats

As most tables need protection from hot plates, it is practical to insulate table mats by quilting them with thin wadding or curtain interlining. For a reversible mat, use a suitable lining or contrasting fabric on the underside.

1 Establish the size of the tablemat and add a 1.5 cm (⅝ in) seam allowance all round. Add another 2 cm (¾ in) all round to accommodate the padding. Cut the top fabric piece, lining or contrasting fabric for the underside, and the wadding to this size.

2 With right sides together and raw edges aligned, place the top piece and the lining/contrasting fabric together. Place the wadding on top of both pieces. Pin and tack in place (fig 6).

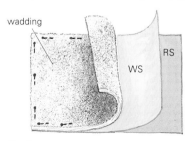

fig 6

3 Stitch around the tablemat through all three layers but leaving a small opening at one end (fig 7). Trim any corners and excess fabric and snip any curves.

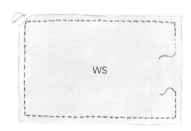

fig 7

4 Turn the mat right side out and lightly press the seam to form a neat edge.

5 Fold in the raw edges of the opening and pin all around the sides to hold the seam flat. Topstitch around the tablemat, being sure to stitch the opening closed. Press lightly.

> AN ATTRACTIVE WAY OF FINISHING
> OFF THESE SIMPLY QUILTED TABLE MATS
> IS TO HAND-QUILT A SMALL DESIGN
> IN THE MIDDLE OR TO ONE SIDE
> OF THE MAT.
>
> ▲

quilted table mats with bound edges

Quilted fabric is commercially available, but it is relatively easy to do your own quilting on a tablemat. The pattern printed on a piece of fabric can be emphasized by stitching along the outlines. For the less adventurous, diagonal lines, tramlines or squares are a simple substitute. Use thin wadding, curtain interlining or quilting. For a reversible mat, use a suitable lining or contrasting fabric on the underside. Bind the edges with bias binding (see page 11).

1 Establish the size of the tablemat and add 2 cm (⅝ in) all round to accommodate the quilting. Cut the top piece of fabric, the lining or contrasting fabric for the underside, and the wadding or quilting to this size.

2 With wrong sides together and raw edges aligned, place the top and bottom pieces together. Insert the wadding or quilting piece between them (fig 8).

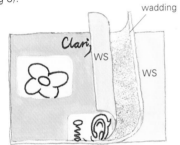

fig 8

3 Using tailor's chalk, mark the quilting pattern of your choice on the top piece.

4 Working along the marked pattern, pin and then tack through all three layers of fabric (fig 9). Stitch along the tacked lines, working from the centre of the mat out towards the sides.

fig 9

ABOVE Colour-coordinated bias binding neatens the edges of this quilted table mat.

5 Trim any skew edges that may have been formed by the quilting and round off the corners of the mat, using a small plate as a guide.

6 Bind the raw edges of the mat with bias binding (fig 10).

WHEN QUILTING INCREASE YOUR STITCH
LENGTH TO PREVENT PUCKERING.

▲

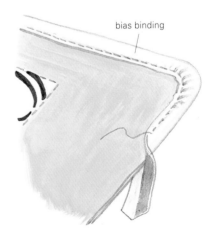

fig 10

nine

lampshades

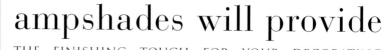

1 ampshades will provide THE FINISHING TOUCH FOR YOUR DECORATING SCHEME. ENHANCE THEIR EFFECT BY COORDINATING THE SHADE WITH THE COLOUR SCHEME OF THE ROOM OR EVEN BY USING OFFCUTS OF YOUR CURTAINING OR UPHOLSTERY FABRIC. THE BASIC DESIGNS CAN BE VARIED BY ADDING DIFFERENT TRIMS AND FINISHES FOR AN INDIVIDUAL TOUCH. MAKING LAMPSHADES USED TO BE A DAUNTING TASK BUT THE SIMPLER, SOFTER SHAPES THAT ARE POPULAR TODAY HAVE ENABLED EVEN THE LEAST-SKILLED NEEDLE-WORKER TO GIVE IT A TRY. THE CRAFT IS QUICKLY AND EASILY MASTERED AND PROFESSIONAL RESULTS CAN BE ACHIEVED IN NO TIME. A NEW, FRESH LAMPSHADE WILL IMMEDIATELY UPDATE THE LOOK OF YOUR HOME FURNISHINGS. CHOOSE THE SHADE FOR THE LIGHT IT CASTS AS WELL AS ITS STYLE, AND BE SURE TO MAKE A CAREFUL CHECK ON THE EFFECT OF LIGHT SHINING THROUGH THE FABRIC. SOME FABRICS CHANGE COLOUR QUITE DRAMATICALLY; OTHERS DON'T LET ENOUGH LIGHT THROUGH. PLAN THE LIGHTING WITH YOUR OWN SPECIFIC NEEDS IN MIND.

OPPOSITE   A whimsical and feminine finishing touch is added to this girl's bedroom by the pretty Tiffany shade, which coordinates with the tablecloth and the bed valance for an altogether romantic look.

150

PLEATED LAMPSHADES

these are simple to make but do require accuracy and concentration. Once the technique has been mastered, the variations are endless. The method below uses fabric, but wallpaper is a suitable substitute. While the scored cardboard bases can be bought, it is easy to make your own. Simply pencil in parallel lines 2 cm (¾ in) apart on a piece of cardboard cut to the correct dimensions. Score along these lines with a craft knife. To sharpen the edges once folded, run the back of the knife along the right side of each crease. Lampshade frames for hanging or standard lamps may be used.

REQUIREMENTS FOR A SMALL SHADE (20 CM [8 IN] HIGH)

20 cm x 120 cm (8 in x 47 in) scored cardboard base | Metal lampshade frame
50 cm (20 in) double-sided fusible bonding material | Bias binding
30 cm x 120 cm (12 in x 47 in) fabric | Fabric glue
30 cm (12 in) diameter metal ring | Paper punch

REQUIREMENTS FOR A LARGE SHADE (25 CM [9¾ IN] HIGH)

25 cm x 150 cm (9¾ in x 60 in) scored cardboard base | Metal lampshade frame
50 cm (20 in) double-sided fusible bonding material | Bias binding
35 cm x 150 cm (14 in x 60 in) fabric | Fabric glue
35 cm (14 in) diameter metal ring | Paper punch

1 Place the fabric right side down on a large, flat surface and press, preferably using a steam iron.

2 Position the bonding material over the fabric, then place the cardboard, scored side up, on top (fig 1).

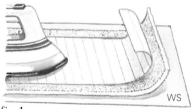

fig 1

3 Press with a hot iron to fuse the card, bonding material and fabric together; it is essential to press the centre down first and then work towards the outer edges.

4 Trim the excess fabric and bonding material from the edge of the cardboard, rolling the card while cutting, as illustrated, in order to get close to the edge (fig 2).

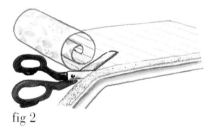

fig 2

5 Very carefully, press again on the right side of the fabric, working from the centre towards the outside.

6 Roll the cardboard up while it is still warm. This will make the application of the bias binding easier.

7 Neatly fold the bias binding over the bottom edge of the cardboard, maintaining a firm hold. Stitch in place, sewing in the centre of the binding and not too close to the edge (fig 3). Repeat to bind the top edge of the shade.

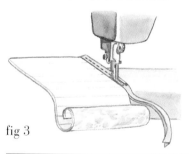

fig 3

WHEN STITCHING, USE A HEAVY-DUTY NEEDLE AND ROLL UP THE CARDBOARD.

▲

8 With the cardboard facing up, pleat the shade concertina-style along the scored lines (fig 4).

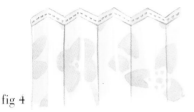

fig 4

9 Working along the top of the shade, punch a row of holes 2 cm (¾ in) in from the edge through the centre of each pleat. Repeat along the bottom edge.

TO FACILITATE ACCURATE PUNCHING, MARK THE PAPER PUNCH WITH MASKING TAPE TO INDICATE WHERE TO LINE UP THE CARDBOARD.

▲

10 Cut very carefully through the fold between alternate holes (fig 5) to form small slots, working from one side of the shade to the other.

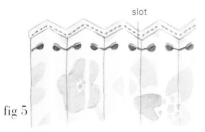

slot

fig 5

11 At the last half-fold, snip from the hole to the side edge, as illustrated above.

12 With the slots facing the inside of the shade, glue the two free side ends of the shade together, placing the snipped end on top (fig 6). Weight the join to hold it in position until the glue dries.

13 Handstitch bias binding around the top ring of the metal frame and the large metal ring, ensuring that the seam lies towards the inside (fig 7).

bias binding

fig 7

14 Pleat up the shade again, and press each fold in turn to maintain neat, crisp edges.

15 Place the shade over the frame. Push the bound top and bottom rings through the slotted holes, dividing the pleats evenly into the three sections of the metal frame (fig 8).

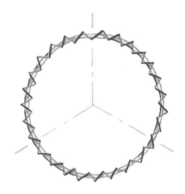

fig 8

fig 6

IF THE BOTTOM RING IS NOT TO BE USED, DO NOT PUNCH A ROW OF HOLES ALONG THE BOTTOM EDGE OF THE LAMPSHADE IN STEP **9**. INSTEAD, PUNCH TWO PARALLEL ROWS OF HOLES 2 CM (¾ IN) AND 3 CM (1¼ IN) IN FROM THE TOP EDGE ONLY. SNIP BETWEEN ALTERNATE HOLES ON THE LOWER ROW ONLY, AND, IN STEP **15**, PUSH THE BOUND TOP RING OF THE FRAME THROUGH THESE SLOTTED HOLES. THREAD A RIBBON THROUGH THE TOP ROW OF HOLES, PULL UP AND TIE; THE TIGHTER YOU TIE THE RIBBON, THE BIGGER THE FLARE OF THE LAMPSHADE WILL BE.

▲

TIFFANY SHADES

these soft, feminine shades are the simplest lampshades to make, and are popular for bedrooms. The cover is elasticated at the top and bottom and can be easily removed for washing. Although the metal frame required for this shade is available in several sizes, the method of construction remains the same.

1 To calculate the amount of fabric required, measure the depth of the frame and add a 13 cm (5¼ in) hem allowance. Measure the circumference of the frame at the widest point (usually the bottom edge) and add a 3 cm (1¼ in) seam allowance (fig 9).

3 If required, attach any lace, trims or frills 8–10 cm (3¼–4 in) up from the bottom edge: hem the frill top and bottom, gather and topstitch onto the shade (fig 10). Ribbon may be added once the shade is attached to the frame.

fig 11

fig 9

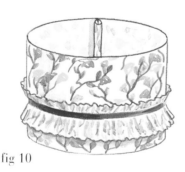

fig 10

2 Cut the fabric to these dimensions and join the short sides using a French seam (see page 9).

4 Stitch a 1.5 cm (⅝ in) double-turned hem along the top and bottom edges of the shade to form two casings, leaving a small opening in each (fig 11). Turn right side out.

5 Pull the shade over the frame and thread elastic through the top and bottom casings, drawing it up so that the shade fits snugly. Secure the elastic firmly. Note that the extra fabric will cover the bottom ring of the frame and will be pulled about 5 cm (2 in) inside the bottom opening by the elastic.

GLOSSARY

GRAIN

The grain of the fabric is the direction in which the threads used to make the fabric are woven. Any fabric will have both a lengthwise and a crosswise grain, and each grain has certain effects on the way the fabric will drape. The lengthwise grain has very little give, while the crosswise grain has more, giving a fuller effect when draped but also stretching more. It is important to consider the effect you wish to achieve and thus the grain required before cutting out the fabric.

BIAS

The bias is the line crossing the two grains of the fabric diagonally. Any fabric that is cut on the bias will have the most stretch of all, which is why binding is cut on the bias.

SELVEDGE

This is the woven strip along each side of a length of the fabric. The lengthwise grain of the fabric (see above) runs parallel to the selvedge.

VELCRO

This is a hook-and-loop fastening tape, which is available in continuous strips of varying widths and is bought by length. One side of the tape consists of hooks and is coarse to the touch, the other consists of soft loops. It is advisable to stitch the soft, looped side of the tape to curtains and blinds which may require washing, as it will not catch on the fabric during laundering. When attaching Velcro to the fabric, stitch the top and the bottom edges in the same direction to prevent puckering. *Press 'n Drape Tape* is a combination of curtain heading tape and Velcro and may be used instead of separate lengths of these tapes.

PIPING

This is a trim consisting of piping cord enclosed in fabric cut on the bias and can be applied to strengthen seams or merely for decorative effect. Piping cords can be purchased in various thicknesses, depending on the desired effect. Ready-made piping can be purchased in various colours and widths, or refer to page 12 to make your own.

FACING

A facing is a piece of fabric which reinforces the main fabric piece. It is stitched to the main fabric piece with right sides together and raw edges aligned and then turned to the wrong side.

GUSSET

A gusset is a panel of fabric inserted between two pieces of fabric to add shape and strength (for example, the side panel of a box cushion cover).

WADDING

Wadding, sometimes known as batting, is cotton or polyester padding used for quilting and upholstery. It is available in various weights and thicknesses.

INTERFACING

This is a light- to medium-weight fabric with little to no give, specially designed to be attached to the wrong side of the main fabric to support it and add stability. Choose the weight and colour of the interfacing to suit the main fabric and the end purpose of the item you are making. Interfacing can be stitched to the main fabric, but IRON-ON INTERFACING is often easier to work with. Iron-on interfacing has a heat-sensitive adhesive material on one side, and is best applied with a steam iron.

BUCKRAM

Buckram is an adhesive stiffening material available in various weights and widths. It is applied to the main fabric by pressing it with a steam iron. For pelmets, use the heavy-weight buckram, which can be purchased in 46 cm (18 in) and 90 cm (36 in) widths. For hand-pleated headings, use the white light-weight buckram which comes in widths of 10 cm (4 in), 13 cm (5 in) or 15 cm (6 in).

FUSIBLE BONDING MATERIAL

This is used to bond two layers of fabric and has heat-sensitive adhesive material on both sides. It is placed between two layers of fabric and then pressed with a steam iron to activate the glue. Fusible bonding material is available in strips or in larger sheets.

INTERLINING

Interlining is fabric intended to be used between the main fabric and the lining to add insulation and to cut out light. It is particularly useful in curtains, but may also be used as padding in tiebacks or to fill goblet headings. Brushed cotton or flannelette may be used instead of interlining.

156

INDEX

Q

R

S

T

U

V

W

Z